WALSHY'S 50 SHADES OF BLUE

by Steve Walsh

Published by
Kkong Events Ltd

Authors
Steve Walsh with John Brindley

CONTENTS

FOREWORD
by Martin O'Neill

Leicester City manager 1995-2000

IT WAS a cold, damp Friday morning in December 1995. I had been manager of Leicester City for less than three days, but already dissention and unrest seemed rife in the camp. The club, relegated the previous season from the Premier League, was stalling in its attempt to regain immediate promotion and their manager Mark McGhee had just left to join Wolverhampton Wanderers. A number of the players felt it was only a matter of time before they, too, would join him at Molineux.

I was hoping that the captain of the team was not in a similar frame of mind. Steve Walsh had been the idol of Filbert Street for a long time. He represented the people of Leicester on the field every Saturday afternoon. His robust, no-nonsense style of centre half play had won the hearts of supporters from the moment he set foot in the door and he was their champion.

I hadn't known Steve at all before my own arrival but, from a distance, I held the same image of him as the supporters did. Still, when a knock came on my office door that particular December morning and Steve walked in saying that he was "in bits", I was taken aback. He had played well the previous Sunday against Norwich and had trained without fuss all week.

He said that he would still travel to Grimsby with the rest of the squad the following day but that he was very pessimistic about his chances of playing. With that, he turned and left the office, leaving me with my own thoughts and suspicions. Maybe this, indeed, was his way of telling me that he no longer wanted to play for the club. Maybe he was genuinely feeling poorly. I really didn't know what to think.

Still in a daze, I noticed that the young physiotherapist Alan Smith had slipped into the office. I told him about Steve's conversation with me a few moments earlier. Alan said that was exactly why he had come to see me. "Don't worry, Steve will play tomorrow. He just needs something to worry about before the game," he told me. Alan was right. Steve played at Grimsby and quite brilliantly for the club for the next four and a half years during my time at the club, mostly preceded by visits to my office to remind me that he was still "in bits".

Steve was a major contributor to the club's success: immediate promotion was won, followed by four consecutive top ten finishes in the Premier League with a couple of League Cup victories, giving the club access to European football for good measure.

A complex character off the field but more than just a warrior on it, he had the ability to play centre forward when the occasion arose and not just for a ten or 15-minute spell at the end of a game when the team was 'chasing' a result. Sometimes he used to venture up field without the manager's permission – but that's another story!

A nasty streak ran through his veins. Quality centre backs possess this vice except most could hide it on the field of play in a more subtle manner than Steve. A record number of dismissals during his playing career seems to bear testimony to that fact.

We would have the occasional chat about missed games brought about by ridiculous suspensions but somehow one felt that Steve wasn't born to be the male chorister in his local church. Anyway, he saw us through many a tough match during that glorious period of Leicester City's history and many a game before, if truth be told.

"Steve Walsh is up there with the best centre backs in the country" was a quotation probably recorded by both of us at some stage of our relationship. Make no mistake, Steve had an ego to go with the best of them. But to reiterate that old saying, Steve could 'talk the talk' and 'walk the walk' in equal measure. He was a big character in the dressing room but, more importantly, a bigger character on the field of play.

Like the rest of us, Steve has had to fight a few demons in his life. We have gone our separate ways these last 15 years but time will not diminish his heroic efforts for Leicester City, particularly those heady days just before the millennium.

He will always hold a special place in the hearts of City supporters. If I met Walshy today, I am sure he would still tell me he is "in bits". With a bit of luck that probably means he will be alright tomorrow.

Good luck, Walshy!

INTRODUCTION
by Steve Walsh

I DEDICATE this book to my fellow professionals, my family – but, most of all, to my faithful Leicester City fans who deserve to know the whole truth.

Walshy is 50 years old, almost to the day, and I have chosen this way of celebrating one of the best relationships of my life. Each and every time I pulled on a City shirt, it was an unbelievable experience – and part of that was my unique connection with you, the supporters. Athough I'm older and greyer today that passion hasn't changed. Not one bit.

It wasn't all great, but never, ever boring. Fantastic victories, heart-breaking defeats, special goals, record sendings off, career-threatening injuries, I experienced the lot during an emotional rollercoaster of a career with the Foxes. That's not to mention all the fun and mayhem off the field which was part of a Leicester City footballer's life in my day.

I was kicked out of Filbert Street back in 2000 and life went from one disaster to another. So much went wrong that I thought I'd fallen out of love with City and with football. I was wrong. I followed City 'here, there and everywhere' on our way back to the Premier League last season and I still enjoy nothing more than watching the lads with the people who care most of all – you, the fans.

You'll enjoy reliving great times here under Brian Little and, particularly, Martin O'Neill. I don't mind telling you that it has often made Walshy, the hard man, very emotional thinking and writing about all we achieved in that era.

There's my take on my greatest ever day against Derby at Wembley, our double League Cup triumph and our phenomenal performances in the Premier League. But you'll feel my pain, too, through countless injuries, red mist and 25 operations!

Yeah, I have many regrets - but those 13 red cards aren't necessarily top of the list. I often felt when taking out my revenge on the pitch, I was doing it for you, who could see what was going on. I paid for it big time through fines and suspensions but the worst punishment was always the thought I may have let you down – and losing the role I treasured as Leicester City captain. Instead my biggest regret is that I spent too much time in that footballer's bubble in which nothing other than the game mattered and neglected my family. That's a failure I'm now actively trying to put right.

Birchy was spot on: I never thought for a second what I'd do when I finished playing football and it caused me hell. Divorce, alcohol abuse, depression, anxiety, bankruptcy and near total breakdown followed when I could no longer rely in 'real life' on that feeling of 'nobody is going to beat me' I had on the pitch. Today's footballers get much better help preparing for their futures when they finish playing, but I still hope many will read this and take my story to heart. Believe me, it's very, very difficult losing the great adrenalin rush of being out there on a football pitch even if you are earning six figure sums per week.

Good news is Walshy's back; I live and work in Leicestershire, notably with my great City mate Muzzy Izzet and my relationship with the football club is better than it's been for years. I've also found new love in my wife Sira, my soul mate who is helping me to both mend the past and build a future, and my family has grown with the addition of young Zaki. I'm so proud of all my children, including Matthew, Nicholas and Olivia, who went through years of torture due to my selfish footballing world.

It's been good fun working with ghostwriter John Brindley, who put away his Forest scarf to help me, over the last 12 months or so. But, make no mistake about it, this is MY story: glory, fuck ups and all. Enjoy it! After all, if you're a Leicester City fan, you've been part of it.

Come on you Blues!

Chapter One
Traitor Taylor

Walshy, you're part of the furniture. Whether as a player, kit man or in the laundry room with Sheila, I want you to be here for years to come.

FUCK ME! Slumped in the passenger seat of my agent Jon Morris's car, the devastating truth began to dawn on me: my Leicester City career was over.

Goals, Wembley visits, injuries, operations, even red cards, flashed in front of my eyes. Nearly 500 games, more than 60 goals and 14 years of service to the club I loved and I was being cast aside like an unwanted trainee; nothing to show except for a bag of boots. No chance to say goodbye to people I stood side by side with over the years, battling for the blue shirt I was so proud to wear.

It was impossible to take in how quickly things had come to this. A few months earlier Martin O'Neill, the great manager who helped me achieve so much, had sat me down in his training ground office. He was planning for the future at Leicester City and genuinely believed we could be an even greater force in the Premier League. Not just a mid-table side who could win the League Cup, but challenging for the top four and the FA Cup, perhaps with a decent run in Europe. After four consecutive seasons in the top ten and, with £11million in the coffers from the sale of Emile Heskey, why not?

He said: "Walshy, you're part of the furniture. Whether as a player, kit man or in the laundry room with Sheila, I want you to be here for years to come." He offered me a new one-year deal and I didn't need asking twice. I would have bled to be involved with Leicester City, especially with Martin at the helm. Part of me felt Martin knew his own destiny and this was his way of saying thanks. I remember standing in the training ground car park with John Elsom, the chairman, and Martin as he delivered the great news to me that I was staying at Leicester City. I was ecstatic; just like the first day I stepped into Filbert Street.

Even after O'Neill moved to Celtic and Peter Taylor, or Tater Peeler as I prefer to call him, took his place, I was assured my future was at City. I will never forget Taylor's words on his first day when he told senior players he would do everything possible to keep the side together and stick to the principles Martin had created over the previous five years (straight out of the window that went). During pre season, we had a team night out at Simon Grayson's club, Undecided, on Churchgate in the city centre, a chance to get to know our new manager away from the training ground. He sat down with me and Muzzy Izzet and began to talk about his plans; yes, he wanted to build on Martin's success and protect the nucleus of the side that had served City so well. I was delighted to hear it. Then Taylor turned to me after our pre-season trip to Holland and said I was in good shape and could play an important part in the coming season. He even promised I would start ahead of Gerry Taggart in the first league game against Aston Villa after the form I had shown both in pre-season and in training. I thought he liked me as I said he could rely on me and I was ready and fit for action, having got over the worst of my injuries.

How wrong could I be? All Taylor's promises proved empty. Instead of being in the team, I wasn't even involved against Villa and then on the bench away at Upton Park against West Ham, which proved to be the very last time I was to pull on a City blue shirt. He completely dropped me from the squad to travel and play Red Star Belgrade, where the lads needed me to lead them into battle. That was the day I knew I had to leave Leicester City. Taylor made it clear he didn't want me around. I'm sure that was because Tony Cottee and I had applied for the manager's job when Martin left for Celtic. He saw us as a threat and couldn't wait to get rid. Tony had been packed off to Norwich; I was next.

I was so out of sorts I almost joined Wolves the previous week. They were just one of the clubs Taylor and co touted to me. Head spinning, I jumped on a train and went to Molineux of all places. At least I found a friendly face there in manager Colin Lee, a bloke I'd got on so well with at City, who invited me for a training session to prove my fitness. I remember, as I was getting changed in the Wolves home dressing room, thinking that perhaps I was sat in the same place as Bully, one of my greatest rivals on the football pitch. Afterwards I sat down with chief executive Jez Moxey and told him, if he wanted me on a month's loan, he'd have to pay me a £10,000 bonus, plus my wages. I said this because I thought they would turn it down but he agreed and I actually shook on it. Only on the train home with Jon Morris did I consider the anger it would cause City fans after the hate-hate relationship I had with Wolves over the years. When I came to my senses, there was no chance.

WALSHY would have made a fantastic Leicester City manager – no doubt about it. I planned to assist him and we had another popular Fox Garry Parker on the coaching side, but we both knew Walshy was the main man.

He was a top player and character; the lads looked up to him. We had no managerial experience but would have built on the great work of Martin O'Neill. We surprised the board with the quality of our presentation but it wasn't to be. They had already settled on Peter Taylor and that proved to be a mistake.

I can understand why Taylor saw us both as a threat but Walshy deserved far better. Things didn't go well for either of us at Norwich; we were commuting and it was never really going to work out. I loved my time at Leicester; I wasn't part of the social circle, as I was still living in Essex, but Walshy was one of the lads who made me feel at home.

We keep in touch when we can and it's great to see Leicester City back in the Premier League.

TONY COTTEE, Leicester City striker 1997-2000

On the train journey home I had a call from TC (Tony Cottee) now playing at Norwich, a club I knew very little about and more than 100 miles away. Cottee said Norwich would offer me a two year contract and, despite great reservations, I agreed to go. I told Taylor I would clear out the few things I had left at the training ground. Even making my way back to Belvoir Drive I couldn't take in the fact I'd never again turn up to train or play for City. I looked around the place and remembered the old shed and the big old gym where we coached kids on a Sunday morning for Jack Curtis. The hard graft I put in on those pitches, even the corner shop where I bought the lads ice-pops after training, flashed back. I wanted to say goodbye to my playing colleagues, the best squad I ever played with. They needed me and I needed them; surely this wasn't happening? Please tell me to wake me up! No more Sheila, the wash lady, Gary, the chef, nor all the girls in the office. It just felt so wrong - come back Martin, please!

It was around 5pm with no one around. Taylor knew this was his big chance to offload me without anyone, including the players and fans, revolting. This was my second home. I loved everything about Leicester City Football Club: the lads, spirit, camaraderie, fantastic fans. Together we shoved green-eyed chants of 'boring, boring, Leicester' down the throats of opposition fans with our regular success and Wembley visits. We loved being unfashionable underdogs. Bring on Manchester United, Liverpool, Chelsea – virtually anybody, but Arsenal – and we'd usually strike a blow for the true spirit of the game. We had the respect of everyone in that league. Nobody took points for granted when they played Leicester City. Now all that was being taken away by someone who'd only been here five minutes and knew fuck all about me or the football club. How dare he come through the door and turn my career upside down just to prove who was boss?

I stepped out onto the street to take another call from Taylor. Abrupt, almost rude, he didn't want me to play for the club again nor be part of his set-up in any way. I was furious. He was ripping my club away from me; the place I'd been so happy for all those years. I told him again I would work hard and fight for my place. But he insisted my horse had bolted. I was thinking about telling Tater Peeler to fuck off. I'd stay, see out my contract and hope he got sacked. But I'm a man whose principles were 'if you're not wanted, move on', so I agreed to leave.

I hadn't done anything wrong yet was being treated like a naughty schoolboy in the corner of the classroom. That was no surprise as Taylor coached grown men like little boys on the training field barking out monotonous instructions. Men who lifted trophies and stood toe-to-toe with the best in the country were doing simple five-yard passing drills.

The club called me earlier that Friday to discuss my loyalty bonus. They were desperate to sell me. Taylor or his assistant Steve Butler - normally the latter as Tater Peeler hated confrontation – used to pull me aside in training to tell me about the latest club that supposedly wanted me. Whether loans, trials or a permanent signing, it didn't bother them in the slightest. By hook or by crook, Taylor wanted me out of sight. I was due a loyalty bonus at the end of my contract for being at Leicester City for 14 years and the manager's agenda was clear: make life so impossible I'd run out the door. City had just paid Tony Cottee his £200,000 loyalty bonus for three years yet simply weren't prepared to make a payment of £90,000 to a guy who'd been there so much longer saying they no longer paid loyalty bonuses if you left the club. I couldn't believe my ears. Not sparing the expletives, I told them to fuck off. I was going nowhere. I felt hurt like never before.

I wasn't wanted and the club was giving me the double whammy of not paying my dues. Despite all my injuries, I still had fuel in my tank and wanted to fight for my place. I ended the call.

Walshy on Tater Peeler: "I've never set eyes on Taylor since I left Leicester City and hope I never will."

I picked up my boots and cleared my stuff into a black bin liner before stuffing it in the back of Jon's car. Emotions began to get the better of me as Jon drove out of the training ground. I hadn't a clue where to go or what to do. So I arranged to meet my mate Pete Welsh for a drink in the New Road Inn on Welford Road.

Over and over in my head I was torturing myself with the thought: why is no one stopping this? Surely chairman John Elsom should have stepped in? How could one man dismantle everything we had worked so hard to build? I almost convinced myself it was just a bad dream; someone would wake me up and tell me everything was going to be alright. Welshy couldn't believe how I had been treated and that I was leaving. When he took it in, we talked about letting the media and fans know. But I didn't want to say anything until I knew the final outcome. I hated the idea that the fans, who took me to their hearts because they knew I was one of them, might think I'd jumped ship for one last pay day. Or perhaps my famous temper had got the best of me and the new manager had no choice? I was often the guy to put my hand up and speak to the media in good times and bad and be as honest as I possibly could. But, right then, when my career and life was at crisis point I made the right decision to keep my mouth closed. Why? Because I knew I'd say something I'd regret. My emotions were so raw. It's taken years for me to really want to talk about exactly what happened. That time is right now because you deserve to know.

For the first time life had no purpose. My mind was completely blank, so much so I honestly forgot totally about Norwich City. I was set to be confirmed as their new signing next day at Carrow Road, joining up with Bryan Hamilton, the manager who took me to Filbert Street in 1986 and was also my boss at Wigan. I should have been happy to be reunited with old friends like Cottee and Iwan Roberts and motivated by the fresh challenge that lay ahead. Norwich was a friendly club and a good one at that. They had faith in me despite my age and injury history and were paying me far more than I ever earned at Leicester. You know what? I couldn't give a fuck about anything or anyone at that very moment and that's the honest-to-Walshy truth.

At 6pm I received the fateful call from Tater Peeler: "Walshy, you can have your loyalty bonus, I've cleared it for you!" What did he want me to say: "Thanks a lot, Peter, that's great news"? It should have been "fuck off, you twat, I'm staying" but I was already committed to Norwich. It was too late now. I felt such a failure I didn't want to go home. I needed to go somewhere familiar, surrounded by friends who wouldn't judge me. Welshy took me to the Midland Hotel on Saffron Lane, Shaun Franklin's place, a man's pub where the lads would be great and not ask any questions. Welshy stayed with me most of the night. The owner promised to keep the place open as long as I wanted. Drink would ease the pain or offer an escape route. Or so I thought. Anyway, I drank myself into oblivion.

The Elvis Presley song *An American Trilogy* was on the jukebox and I played it over and over again. A combination of the emotional words, alcohol and my depressed state of mind left me sitting head in hands, crying. However hard I tried to fight or pretend this wasn't happening, I had to admit defeat and let out my feelings. The lyrics were describing my situation - Elvis was singing about me. I couldn't stop repeating the line 'Oh I wish I was in Dixie, away, away; In Dixieland I take my stand to live and die in Dixie.' The blokes at the bar must have thought I was crazy. Every time I hear that song I still get very emotional just like when I see the Derby winning goal. Get in!

That's how I felt about Leicester City Football Club. I didn't want to play for anyone else. Leaving the Foxes wasn't losing a job, it was a divorce. Looking at it logically, onlookers may have thought I was an ungrateful sod. I still had my family, health and a career to look forward to in a game they'd give their right arms to be a part of. Plus I had so many fantastic memories nobody, not even Taylor, could take away. But that meant nothing to a man who was totally broken.

I continued drinking through the night; never slept a wink. Next thing I knew it was around 7am on Saturday. Missed mobile calls appeared through my drunken haze. My wife Debbie left numerous voicemail messages, as had Jon Morris. No one knew where I was; not my family, friends, nor my new employers Norwich City. I grabbed a bacon sandwich from a nearby café as I'd barely eaten a thing in the last 24 hours. But I still wasn't ready to face people. What could I do? Should I call Jon and dash to East Anglia? The answer should have been 'yes' but, in my state, I couldn't even remember the question. Anyone got a pint?

The phone never stopped ringing, but I couldn't be bothered. I was in no fit state to travel. I was too emotional to deal with a large crowd in unfamiliar surroundings. I was in severe shock and, to this day, don't think I have ever totally got over it. Maybe never will. Writing about it even now brings out a strong emotional reaction from me…

Jon filled in the conversations he had with Norwich during those missing hours. Having received a call from Norwich asking what time to expect me, he contacted Debbie who broke the news I was AWOL. Panic set in before, loyal as ever, he hatched a plan to play for time.

Norwich were told the Walsh family had set off and would be there in plenty of time for kick off. Later he reported I had broken down and was awaiting recovery; the alibi mushroomed into an inefficient recovery company taking us all back home and refusing to give me a forwarding lift to Norwich. The white lies to get me out of the shit, eh!

Somehow I got away with it. Norwich bought the story hook, line and sinker and delayed the announcement of my signing until later in the week. That was very good of them. Sadly for the Canaries, though, the damage was already done. My heart could never be at Norwich City.

Let's go back to the start and I'll tell you why.

Chapter Two

Enter the Hell's Angel

I tasted success with a team I cared
about and wanted more

I've spent a lifetime working in local football and brought young Steve up with memories of the guy I call Sir Thomas Finney and his Wembley appearances. Little did I know that I'd end up with more Wembley memories of Steve, starting with the Freight Rover success with Wigan and almost annual visits there with Leicester City.

Parents are usually biased but it was easy to see Steve's potential from his early years, whether banging goals in or taking his place in defence.

It was a big move for Steve when he left 'home' and went to City, but both Mum and Dad were right behind him. We've kept regular scrapbooks of all his exploits since and know a lot of the personal struggles and heartache he went through to carry on playing. Reading his medical reports is not for the faint hearted. I miss watching him play, travelling to Filbert Street and meeting all the other players' dads. I wish he had stayed in the game as he had a lot to offer football with over 20 years experience - but that's life.

We are a very close family. Mum, Dad and sister Susan are so, so proud of Steve and the love Leicester City fans, in particular, have for him.

EDDIE WALSH, Steve's Dad

CALL ME the 'miracle' who almost went wrong from the very start. Rival fans accused me of being a fat so-and-so and, considering I was a whopping 9lb 10oz when I came bundling into the world at Sharoe Green Hospital, Fulwood, in Preston, on November 3 1964, it's difficult to argue! In all honesty, it was no laughing matter. Partly because of my size, it was touch and go for Mum Jean and me for a while. I wasn't breathing for a few minutes – or so I'm told – and Mum was bleeding badly and needed to stay in hospital for a full month. She couldn't hold me for a full week, so I was sent to the 'bad boys' room in the hospital because of my constant crying. Not the last time....!

Mum and Dad had just about given up on the idea of having children. Infact Mum was told she would never have kids and was sorting out the adoption of Susan when she found out, to her shock and delight, she was pregnant. She kept the good news from the authorities and very soon the Walsh household doubled almost overnight from two to four.

I've never been away from hospitals for long but wasn't so brave back then. Mum tells me I was so unhappy about having my ruptured stomach muscle looked at that I screamed, shouted and slid on the floor so I was taken home. Eventually I was brought back and went under the knife for the first time at the age of 18 months.

More happily, I showed decent football ability from the age of just two belting the ball back to Dad. Another stroke of luck was that Dad was and is an absolute football nut. He was associated with local football side Ribbleton Avenue Old Boys for more than 65 years, winning a special medal for his services to youth football in Preston and becoming a huge influence on my future career. He watched me as often as he could, starting with my early games at Wigan whilst Mum, being too scared, preferred to find out how I was getting on second hand, perhaps through the TV or radio. She, too, however has always backed me 100 per cent and insists I was always an 'angel' and not the 'Holy Terror' she read of in the Leicester Mercury when I was going through my disciplinary problems.

Watching Ribbleton play each weekend wasn't pretty, but a great part of my largely happy childhood. It was good typical working class park football. I spent hours with Dad putting up and taking down the nets but my real memory wasn't of towering headers or sliding tackles. Instead what stayed with me longest was the smell! Ellimans Universal Muscle Rub was a white cream the players rubbed on their legs. Being among the kit, the smell and the 'adult' language, I couldn't have been happier.

Dad worked for British Aerospace pretty much all of his life as a lathe turner. He helped build Tornado Aeroplanes, making nuts and bolts for planes, and absolutely loved it. He had only 13 weeks off for sickness in more than 50 years and showed incredible dedication. That loyalty was a characteristic he instilled in me. He taught me to honour agreements, stick to my morals and treat people the way I expected to be treated. I like to think I lived up to that in my football career – unless someone hit me first, of course! I looked forward to Dad coming home every night with his Daily Mirror so I could fill in the crossword. When he bought the Sunday People, I studied all the Saturday results and league positions for hours. Trust me, I could remember every score.

Mum worked for Uncle Stan, a fishmonger who also had a fruit and vegetable stall. I saw her most days on my way home from school and she always had these huge carrier bags full of potatoes in her hands. She was a grafter, no doubt about it, just like her dad before her. Eventually, she changed jobs and starting working at Preston Royal Infirmary where she also gave long term and highly valued service. Susan was born almost exactly a year earlier than me on November 5th 1963 and still lives within eight miles of our family home. As I say, Susan was adopted, but has been nothing but a true sister to me and we have been very close throughout our lives even though we don't see each other as much we'd like to.

We were a working-class family, without being poor, as Mum and Dad worked as hard as possible to ensure food was on the table. We were well dressed and could do all the things we wanted. Everything we had came from their hard work, a virtue I'll always be grateful for. To be fair, all I can remember wanting to do was to play football and have football gear. I'll never forget Dad getting my first proper pair of football boots from Willie Cunningham, a local football legend who played for Preston and Scotland. He ran his own sports shop and the boots I had my eye on were Adidas Santiagos. They were black and white; the type I still believe professionals should wear. I did actually have a pair of white Alan Ball boots, but they were never going to look right on a young, northern centre-half!

Socially, I was quite an active child, always out with my mates. Best friend Steven Brierley was always by my side. Steven was younger but lived at the top of my road and went to the same school. I idolised him and couldn't wait for him to get back; I would gobble down my food, then go to his house where I'd feast my young eyes on his very good looking mum! I never sat still and didn't want to stay around the house. Steven and I were close, but that didn't stop me from being competitive when we played games. I launched the Monopoly board into the air if I lost; if it looked like he was winning, I'd trick him into something to get me back into the game. I was a bad loser even then and still am today when I don't even like my own children beating me at anything. As for Steve, we're still best mates to this day but I don't see him much.

My short but sweet time in education began at Savick Primary School, where I enjoyed playing football and had my first 'sending off'. Dad recalls I was about eight years of age when I was 'sin binned' for ten minutes in a match – that's the way they handled discipline at such an early age rather than actually dismissing players. School aside, my first ever team was London Road Labour Club where we didn't win a single game in my first season at Under 11s level. Our home ground was a gypsy field and each time we turned up on a Saturday the changing rooms had been messed around with, either burnt down or left with horse shit everywhere. The pitch was in an absolute state. We were thrashed week in, week out, by older lads but knew we were building something special. Within a year we sealed the title and had a real team togetherness with every player understanding his job and what was required. I loved that feeling. I tasted success with a team I cared about and wanted more. Dad recalls I was naturally physical and competitive in my approach, which won't surprise too many people, and that I played both as a striker and an outside left as well as in defence.

I had a mixed time at Ashton-on-Ribble High School, where I wasn't a bad lad in class, but struggled to concentrate. I tried to listen to teachers explaining some theory or presenting a problem, but was always daydreaming about something else. Teachers wrote in my reports that I had ability, but lacked concentration and application. I loved PE, quite liked geography and got an 'O' level in art, a subject in which I showed some talent. I remember one painting I did called *After Monet*, which looked great and has been treasured by Mum on her wall ever since. She still says to everyone 'look what our Steve did when he was at school'. Sorry, Mum, but the honest truth is my teacher did most of it!

I was ok at maths, but didn't like algebra and could never stand physics. I looked forward to school and had no problem getting up in the mornings. I struggled in the afternoons, but that was due to the massive meat and potato pies and coffee Renoir cakes we would scramble out of the gates to buy at lunchtime. They were more like slabs of cake; they were incredible! I ate absolute rubbish – never getting enough of pies, sweets, ice cream and custard cakes. My football career was a great help for my diet, but I suppose in recent years I've slipped back into the habits I had as a child and lost my discipline; blame Tater Peeler!

I got my first taste of professional grounds when winning cup finals for the school and Preston Schoolboys at North End's Deepdale and Blackpool's Bloomfield Road respectively. Selecting the Preston team was my namesake, Steve Walsh senior who, ironically, went on to great success with Leicester City as assistant manager and head of recruitment before moving with Nigel Pearson to Hull City and back again to Leicester City today where he is hugely respected. Some honestly thought the reason Steve picked me was because we were namesakes, but that was nonsense as I was playing to a decent standard. Steve was a great help when I was a youngster and I'm proud to still be in touch with him. When I get the chance, I still like to pop down to Belvoir Drive to say hello, usually with Nigel cheekily introducing us as a father and son combo! Walshy Senior owes me one for answering all the mistakenly sent calls, messages and mail from confused agents and fans.

Rugby was healthy competition for football at secondary school. I really enjoyed the physical side of the sport but my main memories were of being a fast running full back. Tacklers snapped at my heels as I ran from the back. Passing the ball rarely came into my mind.

Something significant happened at the age of 13 – I had my first fight! The argument was over a chocolate bar and involved a couple of bullies picking on a mate of mine. The bullies were a couple of years older than us but that didn't stop me wading in with my left hand and giving them a smack. It did wonders for my reputation and also saved my friend from a likely beating. Generally I got myself into a fair few more scrapes than I ever let on to my parents and ended up outside the headmaster's office more than once.

My love life was pretty low-key as sport was my passion. I remember really liking a girl called Dawn Spark and we shared a few kisses, but we were just kids. My first real crush was an art teacher called Miss Fuller. She was a very attractive brunette in her 20s and, let's put it this way, I soon realised I was becoming a man whenever I was near her. My first serious dates were around the age of 16 or 17. I fancied a few girls but was too busy playing football to care too much.

There were really good players in our school team who were on a par with me when we were kids. I often wonder why lucky people like me make it as professionals whilst the vast majority fall by the wayside. Talent is probably not the number one answer. I'd say it was my focus that gave me the edge. From a very early age, I wouldn't allow anything or anyone to get in the way of my football. Sounds extreme, but that's the way it had to be.

On Sundays I turned out for Lytham St Annes YMCA from under-11s level right through to under-16s, mostly playing at left back. I remember scoring a winner in a cup final at Bloomfield Road against Bispham, a team including Steve Thompson, a future team mate at Leicester City. I turned on a sixpence and netted with my left foot in the top left corner. I'm sure Thommo remembers, even if no one else does!

Blackpool invited me to Thursday night training sessions. Jackie Chapman scouted me on behalf of manager Alan Ball, the England World Cup legend and the great man behind those white boots! I always trained hard as Dad often bought me a fish and chip supper as a reward. Ball signed me on non-contract forms, as they were called then, when I was 15 and I had a year with them, training with the first-team including Paul Stewart, who went on to success with Tottenham Hotspur and Liverpool. My strongest memory of Blackpool, apart from the presence of Bally, was the Squires Gate training ground. We all loaded into this old style bath after our morning's work but once first team goalkeeper Ian Hesford got out just as some of us were clambering in. He'd left a big log floating in there. Just imagine the banter as we scrambled for safety.

Being in such company was tough and quite an eye-opener. Yet football-wise I didn't feel I was given a proper chance to develop and, by the age of 16, I was released. Dad recalls that chief scout David Johnson had brought in a couple of promising youngsters in my position and told him: "Thank you very much, Mr Walsh, but I don't think your son is going to make it at this level." Rejection is always tough but I took the blow pretty well. It was no great issue as, deep inside, I somehow knew I would prove him wrong.

I was soon in for a second rude awakening. My first football love, I have to admit, was Preston North End, the club Dad took me to watch on the terraces. It was there from the age of five that I began to fall in love with the professional game cheering on a good Second Division side including Mike Elwiss and Alex Bruce up front and Roy Tunks in goal. My perfect Saturday wouldn't be complete without getting my meat and potato pie then standing up on the terraces next to the Kop. Then, after the game, watching the fights on the way home with Dad in Moor Park, particularly after the local derby against Blackpool.

Dad told me stories about Preston hero Tom Finney and Stanley Matthews, leaving the youngster convinced that our Tom was number one by a mile. I always wanted to play for Preston, so having a short trial at Deepdale, where my football dreams began, was fantastic. That was until sober reality kicked in. I was so disappointed.

I had a week at Preston and it seemed they didn't even know I was there. Nobody said anything or even acknowledged me, so I simply walked out on them. I was ambitious but wasn't going to waste time with people not interested in what I had to offer.

Yes, it really was third time lucky. First, though, a Blackburn Rovers scout came to visit our family home to try to persuade me to sign but I was more interested in Wigan Athletic. I was offered a trial with the Latics with the sweetener I'd be playing in the B team on the Saturday. There, after two false starts, I finally found a club that suited me. I was working as an upholsterer and carpet fitter and travelling to training after a full day around the town. It wasn't easy, but I never complained. If I hadn't made it as a player, I could happily have ended up doing that job long term. It was good, honest labour to keep me grounded and money coming in whilst I worked hard to develop my football career. I was working all day in all sorts of places sometimes working late preparing nightclub floors nailing plywood 4" centres for just £21 a week. I ended up working out of the back of a lorry for Keith Astbury at True Line Upholsterers in Preston, stripping suites ready to be upholstered. Sometimes it was so cold I could barely feel my fingers. I remember struggling to cut this material with scissors before they realised they had given me right-handed scissors when I was left-handed. No wonder everything took me so long! I was springing and webbing and lifting suites up and down stairs. I worked so hard during the day that some evenings I could barely lift my feet up, let alone run myself ragged on a cold and wet training ground, but somehow I found the energy. More seriously, I had a narrow escape when I went 40 feet up a ladder to try to fix a blind at a Ministry of Defence building. In my haste I didn't think about the dangers of a wooden floor and suddenly the ladder, I had climbed up on my own, gave way. As it slid down the wall, I jumped off at the last moment to soften the blow and wasn't badly injured, but it cost the boss more to put things right than we made for the job. I also remember having four stitches in my forearm after slipping with a Stanley knife. Those were just two early examples of accident prone Walshy.

I may not have been that confident with women as a teenager but my ability to handle myself was growing as an incident in Preston when I was 17 years old showed. I used to enjoy a lager and black in the Black Bull with Ian Carter, a boxer mate. One night a girl was taking Ian, my friend Chris Hixon and me back home in a red Metro when I realised we were being followed. This car overtook us, stopped and suddenly we were surrounded by four massive blokes. We urged the girl to drive on but she panicked and we were dragged out of the car into the middle of the street. One of the big boys confronted us but Ian jabbed him until his nose was all over the place. We were outnumbered so decided to run but I had my beige 'pulling' shoes on so it was difficult to get away. I turned to face my aggressor and, as he came close, smashed him full in the face with my left hand and he fell straight over. Then I sorted the next bloke out who was kicking Chris before joining Ian to finish the job. I felt proud our first battle was a win. No doubt about it young Walshy was definitely more Holy Terror, or even Hell's Angel, than angel – good job Mum didn't see the full picture!

Chapter Three

Filling Big Lloydy's Boots

I stuck my foot up to block the ball
and deliberately kept my studs up

NO MATTER how good you are – and I was no Lionel Messi or George Best, let's face it – you can't do it alone. Everyone needs special people to help you along the football road; people prepared to give you a chance or words of advice that stick with you for life. I was lucky in my career to come across several such folk. With my disciplinary record – and I collected more than my share of red and yellow cards before I ever arrived at Leicester City – it would have been very easy for a manager to give up on me. I was more than fortunate with the quality of guys who stuck with me.

Larry Lloyd, player manager of Wigan Athletic, was my first boss and a huge influence on my career. Similarities between us were so clear, nobody could have missed them. He, too, was a big left sided centre back who knew how to handle himself on the football field. Lloydy regularly ran the gauntlet of referees and managers at Liverpool, Coventry and Nottingham Forest. Yet he stayed on the rollercoaster long enough to enjoy the best years of his whole career under Cloughie after others had written him off. Excuse me if I don't mention those European Cups!

My first major influence however at Wigan was first team coach Harry McNally who, along with Dave Crompton, was in charge of the youth team. Harry was something else but not in the same way as Miss Fuller! Sergeant Major-like and a throwback to a previous era, Harry took to me because I was hard working and never complained about anything.

Looking back now, I can clearly see how the Wigan experience shaped the Walshy, City fans remember; even then, I knew no fear, drank hard, played hard and never knew when I was beaten.

The teenager who walked into Springfield Park knew little more about alcohol than those lager and blacks and the odd pint of beer Dad bought me at the Bulls Head in Preston. Walking into a 'team bonding' session early in my stay with the club was my very first taste of the drinking culture that was part of being a professional footballer during my career. For Harry and Larry, it was a chance to enjoy each other's company.

There was Lloydy with fellow European Cup winner John Robertson and Les Bradd, the former Notts County striker, sitting together at the bar in the Boars Head in Wigan. Every round would be the same; the trio, all with a fag in their hand, ordered a half of beer and a short from the top shelf. They were soon rolling around with laughter - in Robbo's case falling off his chair altogether. So this was the way top footballers socialised! Opting out wasn't an option. Young striker Mike Newell didn't touch the hard stuff at all and far preferred a pint of milk. When he asked for his favourite pint, Lloydy just turned to Graham Barrow, one of our senior players and roared: "Graham, get him a fackin' beer!" Newell placed it out of the way and returned to the bar for a soft drink only for Harry to scream at him to drink the beer - still he wouldn't touch it. Newelly could have done with a few lessons on how to handle his drink. When he turned 26, he was forced to start drinking by Everton boss Howard Kendall, who knocked back the hard stuff for fun. Needless to say, Newelly now loves a few beers.

Harry was a stonemason and proper old school. On my debut I remember him teaching me a very important defender's trick - "miss the first header and head the back of his fackin' head and get a few stitches!" Harry was exactly what I needed. There was loads of physical contact in football in the early 1980s and being shy wasn't an option. I had to learn the real art of being a centre half if I wanted to make it.

David Lowe, later to play alongside me at City, regularly went for extra training sessions with me and Harry on Thursday nights. We were definitely his favourites and he invested a great deal of time working with us. He insisted I wore studded boots on an Astroturf pitch - and they were rugby-style massive - whilst Dave wore nice comfy Adidas Copa Mundial trainers. Crazy when you think about it but that was Harry's way. He wanted his centre backs to be tough. Lowey turned me inside out in return for a good kicking.

I was beginning to emerge as a dominant centre half in Wigan's reserve team, almost always watched by Dad. One highlight from my youth days was facing up to Mark Hughes and Norman Whiteside in Manchester United's all-star 'A' team. Throughout this time I was very grateful to Dave Crompton. He was a great help in my development as a player and as a man.

My first team chance came completely out of the blue when I was still working part time as an upholsterer. Sat in the stands admiring a top class Manchester City side being held to a notable 1-1 draw by Lloydy and co in the first leg of a Milk Cup tie, I hadn't a clue I'd be playing in the return at Maine Road. I was none the wiser even after travelling with the team to Manchester. It was nothing new for Lloydy to take painkillers to nurse the back that troubled him during the latter part of his career but, on this occasion, he just couldn't make it. When he walked out onto the pitch, he put his arm around me and told me I was playing…. shit! I thought he was joking. I was taking the place of a former England international defender and turning out against a team boasting Joe Corrigan, Paul Power and Asa Hartford among their many stars. My job was to blot out the might of new signing David Cross and Kevin Reeves. I had no time to prepare or come to terms with the occasion – but that was Lloydy's idea. He didn't give me time to doubt myself although I was extremely nervous just before the big kick off. I wasn't the only teenager in the side – my youth team mate David Lowe also got his chance in place of injured top scorer Eamonn O'Keefe. On the other side of the coin we had the vast experience of former Scotland skipper Archie Gemmill in midfield.

City predictably won 2-0 to knock us out of the cup with two goals from Paul Power yet we held our own for long periods and I had a blinder. Lloydy's words made me feel 10 feet tall: "He played out of his skin… for Walsh to make his debut against a First Division side and hardly put a foot wrong speaks volumes for the lad." I'm sure Lloydy saw something of himself in me. Perhaps he took a liking to a youngster who was headstrong yet wanted to learn. Either way, I'll always be grateful to him as the first manager to give me my big chance – and the first to fight my corner when the going got tough.

Soon afterwards I came down to earth with a bump during a midweek trip to Exeter as I got my first professional red card in only my second Football League game. We were badly hit through injuries with five youngsters in the starting line up and I got myself in a tangle with experienced striker Steve Neville, on loan from Sheffield United. Neville pushed me and I retaliated by swinging an arm at him. I must have missed by a good six inches but the home player dropped like a stone.

To make it worse still, we lost 2-1. Afterwards I got a taste of Lloydy's tongue for the very first time. I shit myself.

For a fair while I continued to combine manual work with playing professional football. Weekends often saw me playing a match on the Saturday and working for Keith whilst my team mates put their feet up. Nevertheless I soon started to feel pretty settled at Wigan especially after Lloyd hung up his boots and I regularly wore the number five shirt. I got a reputation for being versatile later in my career but wasn't quite so happy when handed the role of emergency goalkeeper at Bury. Our usual number one Roy Tunks, my former Preston hero, was injured, so I went between the sticks with the score 1-1. I got myself into trouble within a few minutes, rushing out of my penalty area for some reason to wipe out their winger and getting a silly yellow card. Then, with just a minute or two to go, Bury won a free kick and I made a bad misjudgement, leaving a shot I thought was flying over the bar and watching it soar into the back of our net for the winner. Lloyd made no concessions for a rookie keeper, stringing me up against the dressing room wall as he ranted at me afterwards.

I was impressing enough in my usual defensive role though for rumours to spread that other clubs wanted me. Instead I signed professional forms for Wigan in August 1983 a couple of months short of my 19th birthday. It was a two-year deal on £90 a week for the first 12 months, going up to £130 in year two. The money didn't mean a thing to me and Mum ensured I kept my feet firmly on the ground. Worried I was spending too much, she insisted I gave her my wages so she could organise everything.

I've won a lot of unlikely battles in my life but few as amazing as our Wigan version of Wacky Races. I'm referring to the unequal challenge I had with Newelly and Graham Barrow driving to the training ground each morning. There were just a few miles between Springfield Park, Wigan's former ground, and Robin Park, now the venue for the DW Stadium. We turned the journey into a race that put Formula One to shame. It should have been no contest. Newell's father was owner of the local Ford dealership, so his son had a sponsored RS Turbo car and Graham wasn't far behind either in his Ford Capri two litre injection. My car was a lot more modest. After passing my driving test a few months earlier and swapping the Mini Dad bought me from my next door neighbour, I'd splashed out a full £50 on a Ford Cortina two litre GT with double headlights from my boxer mate Ian. I loved that car. It had a Leicester City-style blue and white stripe and looked like something from Starsky and Hutch. It was a flying machine and I drove it like Michael Schumacher!

My rivals stopped at the red lights but I'd go careering through, ignoring the signals and using every possible part of the road to gain an extra edge. This was where I had a vital advantage; for whereas, Newell and Barrow didn't want me near their super sporty cars, I couldn't give a shit. All that bothered me was getting to the finishing line first – because I hated losing. It looked like a scene from *America's Dangerous Drivers* and must have been a nightmare for other road users innocently going about their daily business. Somehow we got away with it without bothering those other boys in blue. I swerved around corners, mounted kerbs and even went down the odd no entry street; winning every time gave me such a buzz. Often the gear stick came off in my hand. I rammed the damned thing back in whilst driving and needed a push start from the lads to get the car going again after training for the 17-mile journey back home to Preston. Club officials hadn't a clue what was going on. They were impressed we all arrived in such good time for training!

We had great fun on our away days. Long trips to places like Gillingham were totally different to the way players prepare for matches today. Overnight stays were too expensive, so we made a seven hour coach trip. That meant endless cards, listening to music on the radio and a midway stop for 10oz steaks! Harry convinced himself that eating steaks before a game would mean "we'd fight like fackin' tigers". We weren't going to try to persuade him otherwise. Colin Methven, my centre half partner who taught me how to head a ball and defend, always carried six cans of bitter for the long trips home on the back of the bus.

A trip to Bradford City's Valley Parade was one of the most memorable. Lloydy was good friends with the rock band AC/DC and lead singer Brian Johnson, along with a couple of band members, regularly sat on the bench. They even joined in team talks in the dressing room. It was unbelievable; we didn't know whether to laugh or cry. On this occasion, Harry was wearing a fur hat and O'Keefe couldn't wait to wind him up. The striker turned to Harry in front of the other lads and AC/DC and asked him why he had a cat on his head? All good fun, you might think, but Harry's cat had died during the week. He stormed off with tears in his eyes and we were meant to go out and play the game afterwards. It was more like a soap opera than professional football.

That was when I first locked horns with another of the game's genuine hard men, Bobby Campbell, playing up front for Bradford. I first came across him before as he was preparing for the match in his usual way with a few whiskeys. The striker with a squeaky voice left his mark on me with a tackle that shattered my shin pad and very nearly did the same to my leg. I went off the field for ten minutes before returning to get my revenge and show him I wasn't scared. I won every header and dominated him with a master class performance. I seemed to rise to the occasion when provoked, as you City fans well know.

I met my match when Larry took us down to Central Park, home of Wigan Rugby League Club. They had top notch facilities and great players. I remember seeing legends like Ellery Hanley and Shaun Edwards – they were absolutely ripped, far different to us. The boss locked us all in the sauna for around 20 minutes to sweat everything off before dragging us out one by one and throwing us into a freezing cold plunge pool. Once I came out shivering and walked back into the changing rooms to get dried and dressed to be confronted by this man giant shouting the odds about someone hanging his clothes on his peg. I was never going to admit it was my stuff lying on the floor in a pool of water. I walked past him and hid in the toilets until he'd gone. When I saw the name 'Bonecrusher' above the peg, I knew I'd made the right call!

A violent temper and not allowing anyone, however intimidating, to get one over on me has always been part of my make-up. Again, I can trace the many well publicised one-to-one battles I had over the years in a Leicester City shirt back to Wigan and a blood curdling dual with Billy Whitehurst. A bricklayer by trade, he was an animal, as hard as nails and a big tank of a striker who always put himself about. Some folk rated him the hardest player ever to play the game. Hate to admit it, but I do too! I came across him playing against us for Hull City at Springfield Park and it took about 10 minutes for me to get the message. The ball was 70 yards away when he head-butted me. I went down on one knee and stayed down for a few minutes. I wasn't thinking how badly I was hurt, but getting him back. He was the first player in professional football whose card was marked – first of many!

Revenge didn't happen that particular day, so onto Plan B, the away match at Boothferry Park. Our coach pulled up just outside the Hull home dressing room, reminding me of the task in hand: get Whitehurst! That was the first time I deliberately elbowed someone and it was a beauty to see his nose bent to fuck. He was furious and spent the rest of the afternoon taunting me and threatening what he was going to do to me afterwards. "I will do you in the bar, you piece of shit," he said. Crunch time – and possibly a turning point in my whole career – came in the changing room after the final whistle. I was chewing over a difficult decision: do I duck out and dive straight onto the coach, or head to the bar to face him out? It was a close call for a teenager confronted with such an intimidating guy but, you guessed it, I went for a drink; Walshy never backs down to no-one. I walked into the room and saw him staring at me. If he was going to do anything, this was his big chance. He walked up to me threateningly with a pint of Newcastle Brown in one hand and a glass of brandy in the other. He slammed his beer on the bar and I thought this is it; my fists were clenched ready for him to lift his hand. Then he asked what I was drinking and the tension was broken. To be fair, I think he respected my bravery at not caving in to him either on or off the pitch. I had plenty of physical tussles with Whitehurst mostly in a Leicester City shirt and would like to think I mostly got the better of a bloke who was a very good player as well as a street fighter.

Another early notch on my hardman CV was Fash the Bash, John Fashanu, then playing for Millwall. My first close encounter with a striker who terrorised defenders with the Crazy Gang ended in me being surrounded by the whole Lions team as we left the pitch at Wigan. I definitely left my mark. It started in the first half when I went up for a header, knocked into him and fell on top of him, puncturing his lung. It was always going to be an awkward fall and I made it as bad as I could for him. The big man was stretchered off and the rest of the Millwall team were in no doubt I did it on purpose. That was one of the first and very few times in my whole career when I heard one team shouting for one of their players to go out and break someone's leg – mine! Their skipper barked out his orders. It was an absolute disgrace. Instead in the last few minutes of the match I made it 2-0 to Walshy. We were pressing for a winner when a Millwall defender shaped to clear the ball up the line and I realised it was their captain. Perfect! I stuck my foot up to block the ball and deliberately kept my studs up. It's a classic football trick and one I'm not usually proud of. But, on the day, I was pleased with myself for getting the better of a team who had no shame in putting themselves about. He went down like a sack of shit and I didn't even get a yellow card. Happy days!
There was a scuffle at the final whistle with angry Millwall players being pulled off me, shades of Wrighty at Filbo years later. I suppose Fash got some measure of revenge when I was sent off in the return game in London. But, again, I left him plenty to remember me by.

Larry and I generally got on very well but one thing we didn't see eye-to-eye over was my love life. I finally 'cracked it' at the age of 17 when I had sex with an old school flame of mine – but that wasn't a problem. The manager took far more notice when he heard I was going out with one of the staff. Yvonne worked in hospitality at Wigan and was absolutely gorgeous - long dark hair, tanned, petite and generally stunning. She was 29 years old, so you can understand why I was flattered. Her husband was in prison and she came to my house in Preston, where

I was still living with my parents, to see me. One of our favourite tricks was to go out to Blackpool where we had sex on the beach, in the gardens, anywhere. I was enjoying myself but Harry and Larry weren't happy. They called me into the office and demanded I stopped going out with her. I knew exactly what was wrong – Larry fancied her too! No way was I going to agree to that one. Altogether we went out for more than a year before nature took its course and I started shagging someone else!

I had to grow up fast on the field. Larry taught me about passing the ball out from the back, hitting the corners of the pitch and gaining territorial advantage. All I could do was find the back of the stand or slice one off the outside of my left peg. Mentors Colin Methven and Graham Barrow taught me more about being a centre half and how to handle myself. They were true warriors on the field and I looked up to them as heroes. Then there was Roy Tunks driving me to training in his old brown Rover. A German, born in Wuppertal, he was a real character. Whenever I think about him, I swear I can hear Peter Frampton's *Baby, I love your way*, the song he played over and over on his cassette player.

I could have joined Chelsea. Ian McNeill, once of Wigan and now John Neal's assistant manager at Stamford Bridge, came to my house almost begging me to sign for the First Division club. Larry told John Butler, David Lowe and I to travel to Chelsea for talks. Chairman Ken Bates was owed £70,000 by Wigan and wanted his money back. The plan was that Bates would get all three of us for free but Larry ordered us not to sign. Bates was throwing his (considerable) weight around to warn Wigan he could call his debt in at any time. After the meeting finished, I put my head down and got up to walk out. Bates called me back and shouted at me for not shaking his hand. But it wasn't a mistake – I didn't trust the bloke. I didn't like him then and never have. Years later he wrote in his programme notes that City came to Chelsea to play for penalties. Martin O'Neill was seething and had the media and general public in stitches when he described Bates as a 'footballing cretin'. And so say all of us!

Lloydy did ok for us but fell victim to our up and down results early in 1983. His days were numbered as he seemed to be quarrelling with the board quite regularly. He was frustrated at not being able to add to his group of players and finding it difficult to keep the higher division vultures at bay. Lloydy's departure meant I spent a short time being managed by the great Sir Bobby Charlton. He took over as caretaker and was wonderful to work with. I was in awe of the bloke to be quite honest. Standing in front of me was a World and European Cup winner and a Manchester United and England legend. I didn't have too many dealings with him, but he pulled me aside in training to have a word about my lack of discipline. He was worried I wouldn't have a future in the game if I kept getting booked or sent off. The guy's quality stood out on the training pitch; he was unbelievable. He thought nothing of pinging the ball straight into the top corner from 30 or 40 yards in shooting practise – nearly 20 years after he won the World Cup. He gave the older lads a nip of whisky before games, but not us youngsters. Who knows how good a manager he could have been given a longer crack at the role? Either way, Sir Bobby is a football man through and through and commands respect worldwide. I'm proud to have worked with him, even if only for a few months.

Harry then stepped up from his role as assistant manager to move into the hot seat. Plymouth Argyle were chasing me and had a couple of bids turned down. You've got to laugh but they made an initial bid, then came back with a second that was £35,000 lower! It didn't matter too much anyway because I wasn't interested. Again, I was grateful for the way Harry protected me when things went wrong. I was sent off in a fiery 3-3 draw at Rotherham United when we finished with nine men, and again at York, for a second bookable offence involving big striker Keith Walwyn, the same week. Harry pointed out that I was young and raw even though he could have done without the suspension problems. To be honest, I was suffering from the same lack of discipline that will be all too familiar to City fans. When things were going against me, I saw the red mist and lashed out. Older and wiser players knew this and wound me up, knowing referees had me marked down as having a hot temper.

Harry lasted about two years before another significant character came into my life when Northern Irishman Bryan Hamilton took over in April 1985 after five pretty successful years at Tranmere Rovers. I thoroughly enjoyed playing for Bryan from day one. He hammered me for my disciplinary record but did it with my best interests at heart. He was the first boss to throw me into a centre forward role, a move that saw me score crucial goals against Derby County and Bristol City as we won our battle against relegation from the Third Division. I also got my first taste of Wembley and silverware. It may have 'only' been the Freight Rover Trophy but that didn't matter. I remember walking around the grand old stadium before the game in our new suits, New Balance sponsored trainers, tracky and boots, thinking this is what I want more of. We beat former Leicester boss Frank McLintock's Brentford 3-1 with spectacular goals from Mike Newell, Tony Kelly and David Lowe to match the surroundings. Lowe and I were paid a £15 appearance fee for our day of glory. We were greeted by thousands on our triumphant return to Wigan and crowds started to increase as a result of our success. Gradually we were becoming a top team.

Wembley glory and our general improvement under Hamilton gave our young side – we had nine players under 21 on our big day – a great platform to launch a promotion bid the following season. Instead things turned in a far different direction. You never know what's around the corner in football. I had every reason to look forward to the 1985-86 season, having been the subject of a £100,000 bid from Charlton and interest from Leicester City, but I wanted to push on at Wigan under a manager I got on so well with. There was talk of Wigan building their side around me and I intended to give Hamilton and co my full backing and see where that took me and the club.

Unfortunately, the answer was to hospital as I received a serious injury in a fairly meaningless pre-season game – and gave my poor parents the shock of a lifetime! The Manx Cup was a traditional curtain raiser in which we ironically had already beaten Leicester City in the Isle Of Man – the only time I ever played against the Foxes at first team level – before I came up against a physical striker in John Thomas as we hosted PNE, my home town team.

There was only local pride at stake but you wouldn't have thought so the way the former Bolton player put himself about. He was elbowing players and sliding in late and had already caught me twice before the incident in question. I think we both knew the referee had lost control by this point and Thomas came in with a diabolical foul, one of the worst I ever witnessed. As I tried to play the ball down the wing, I was taken out from the side and that's when the dark comedy started with the physio. First, he tried to stand me up which was never going to work as I collapsed in agony. Then the doc put an injection in my right leg. I just had enough life left to scream that it should have been my left. I had broken my tibia and fibula and was stretchered off by St John Ambulance staff. What Dad, uncle Stan, cousin Roy, along with sis Sue and family, who were all watching, didn't know, was that at almost the same moment a spectator collapsed on the terraces. We only had one stretcher at Wigan so they had to tear down a billboard and carry the poor guy away. It soon became obvious his condition was very serious and he was first for the ambulance. Dad arrived from the stand just in time to see the ambulance driving away and asked a copper if I was ok? "No, I'm sorry, he's died!" was the reply. So, for an agonising 20 minutes or so until he saw me in the flesh, Dad thought the worst. There's nothing you can do but laugh about it now although it was a real life tragedy for one family.

Being out for goodness knows how long was new territory for me and very hard to get my head round. I worried if I would ever be the same again. I was in full length plaster for 12 weeks and traction in hospital for 11 days. Injured players certainly weren't mollycoddled at most clubs in those days and it was a lonely and very difficult journey back to fitness. I missed the majority of that potentially important season but was really grateful for the support of the majority of that Wigan side who took the time and effort to visit me in hospital. That tells you something about the closeness we had at Springfield Park. Graham Barrow did his very best to raise my spirits and get me into trouble at the same time – putting a porn film on my bedside TV, then deliberately leaving the remote control out of reach, so the nurses got an eyeful when they came to see me. Also, my leg that was in traction accidently got upset by James, his young lad, pulling the weights and almost sending me through the roof with pain. I stayed as fit as I could taking calcium tablets washed down by plenty of Guinness to speed up my recovery, as you do.

I made it back before the end of the season – my first appearance being against Leicester City Reserves, of all teams, at Springfield Park - before being used up front by Hamilton as we produced a stirring performance before being pipped for the third and final promotion spot by just a single point by Derby County. Annoyingly, the Rams had three games left after we finished our programme and a couple of wins turned things their way. Needless to say, nothing like that would be allowed nowadays. I thoroughly enjoyed playing for Wigan – and still have a lot of affection for them - but we'd probably gone as far as we could. In fairly rapid succession we sold our main goal threats in Mike Newell and David Lowe, who both featured in the next chapter of my football career, and Warren Aspinall. Had we kept them, Derby might still have been down and out. So cashing in on their promising young centre half wasn't too much of a surprise.

This was an exciting time for me off the field for now I had a pretty blonde in my life. Debbie Steele was my first 'real' girlfriend in the sense that I hadn't been serious about anyone before. Previously I loved and left them which suited me fine as my career was my number one priority with nothing else getting in the way. But Debbie was different. I was out on a Christmas do with John Butler when my eyes spied this smallish blonde woman and we got chatting. She had no reason to feel in awe of me as a footballer as she had a good job as a secretary and was a year older. We got on well and began dating whilst both of us were still living with our parents.

Once we'd been going out for a year or so, we started to make plans – always including a place for football, of course. We got wed in the early summer of 1986 at English Martyrs RC Church in Preston and honeymooned in Palma, only a few miles away from the rest of the Wigan lads. Strange co-incidence, eh? They were enjoying an end-of-season break in Magaluf to get over our heart-breaking end to the season.

Getting married brought with it a new house on Blackpool Road, Preston, which I renovated from top to bottom. Somehow I hopped round all the debris with my leg still in plaster tiling walls and filling skips, as I was a bit of a handyman. Not sure what the club thought, but I was doing my very best to get the two of us off to a good start. Step by painful step I got that property ready for us to live in but we never made it through the front door. Instead football took a fateful hand again and I'm so glad it did. I was about to sign for Leicester City and become a First Division footballer!

Chapter Four

Fabulous Filbo

> " It was like sex but a million times better "

STRANGE how things work out, isn't it? One moment I was concentrating on domestic bliss and getting back onto the pitch with Wigan Athletic, next, my life was going in a completely different direction. Yet I had the feeling this was meant to be. I was sad leaving the club, who gave me my first major break in football, in football, but it was harder to leave the area where I was brought up. As always, Mum and Dad were firmly behind me, reassuring me I wasn't going to the other end of the world.

Gordon Milne was the first Foxes manager to ask about me whilst guiding City to a modest First Division finish in the 1985-86 campaign. Events then took a surprise turn to make the transfer happen. Milne never won the hearts of City fans so the club tried to help him out. Rather than replace him altogether, City used Milne's football brain in the role of general manager – the equivalent of Director of Football in today's money – and brought in a younger guy in his place. That man was none other than Wigan Athletic's Bryan Hamilton, who had done nothing to harm his CV at Springfield Park.

Milne had already made a very important signing in Ipswich Town's Russell Osman in central defence but the club was looking for extra cover alongside Irishman John O'Neill, who divided opinion among the fans. It wasn't too difficult for Hamilton to persuade Milne I was his man as I was already on his radar. Partners often get the rough end of the deal in such circumstances but it was great that Debbie happily accepted us upping sticks to move to the Midlands just three days before we were meant to move into our 'dream' house.

To be honest, she didn't have much choice. I would have moved heaven and earth to play First Division football and gone on my own if I had to.

Hamilton picked Debbie and I up from Preston and drove us over to Filbert Street to take a look at the club. I'd like to say I got goose bumps walking into Filbert Street for the first time but that honestly wasn't the case. I was coming to Leicester completely blind. I knew nothing about the club other than they were in the East Midlands and in the top division where I wanted to be. The only link I'd had was collecting a few football cards with Leicester players on – although, the great Gordon Banks apart, I didn't know too many names. Frank 'Elvis' Worthington and Keith Weller headed the list of recent legends I was to get to know, along with Birchy, but had very little knowledge of when I arrived.

I remember leaving the M6 in Brian's Mercedes, seeing a sign saying M69 to Leicester, then driving along the long Narborough Road. I kept looking for the Filbert Street floodlights as we drove past Frank Berry scrap metal trains and feasted my eyes on the 'Statue of Liberty' monument at the top of the building on the corner. Then there was the iconic Bentleys roof, from which I later saw fans watching us in action. The ground itself was much bigger and better than I was used to although I'd had a brief taste of the big time playing at Maine Road and Wembley. Our talks were almost comical but the way most football clubs probably did their business. I was in and out of the manager's office four or five times trying to strike a deal with Milne. Graham Barrow told me to talk to them but sleep on it for 24 hours before I made a decision. Agents were still fairly new to the game and I didn't have one, which didn't help. All I had to go on was that Wigan promised to put both David Lowe and I on the same money as the highest paid player if we signed our new deals. It was pure guesswork, but we didn't expect to get much more than £150 a week.

The way it worked was this: Milne told me what the club was prepared to offer and jotted a few figures down on a piece of paper; I said my piece and he threw the paper in the bin and started again. After a while, the bin was almost full to overflowing with useless scribbled notes. I was playing games as I'd have happily signed for nothing. I know that's easy for me to say, having later earned some good contracts as a footballer, but the financial side meant nothing at the time. I wanted to play with and against the best players in the land. My first City deal, however, was a good one. I signed for a fee of £100,000 on a four-year deal at £300 a week going up by £50 every year. I also got a £3,000 a year signing on fee and £10,000 to relocate, which was great. Checking into the Holiday Inn, I lived the high life before realising £10k would run out quickly that way. From there, I moved to the Du Val Hotel on London Road, where I stayed for most of my first year at the club, before buying a house in Barwell, Hinckley. It was a friendly place where I got to know owner Mick Navarro, a massive drinker and gambler, mad on his horse racing, along with his brother Willie. Among the other tenants was goalkeeper Paul Cooper, who joined City from Ipswich Town. He took me under his wing and became a good mate.

I'll always remember my first day at Leicester City. Our Belvoir Drive training ground was out of action and we were working at Leicester University on a really hot day. It was a fantastic feeling knowing I was a First Division player. We all went on a three mile run in the Uni grounds. Very good at sprints and hill running, I always struggled with long distance running and three miles was a fucking long way for me, believe me. Also, as the only person I really knew at the club was manager Bryan Hamilton, I felt more than a little out of my depth.

Settling into the club wasn't easy. Walking into a new dressing room for the first time is quite intimidating and certainly was for me. I could handle myself on a football pitch but was quite shy and withdrawn off it. I hated not knowing anyone and felt really embarrassed. That's just the way I am until I get to know everyone and come out of my shell. I wasn't the life and soul of the party from day one. Training was fairly simple with a lot of five-a-sides in which Hamilton and Milne sometimes took part. Milney loved a five aside and that's about all he did. That was as close as they got to being a partnership. There was tension between them and it didn't seem to work for either. Milney was probably disillusioned at having a manager brought in above his head and Hamilton would have preferred a clean start. It was only a matter of time before they would oust Milney. Probably the biggest impression Milney made on me, apart from his five-a-sides, was his drinking. During a trip to Sweden, he handed a bottle of brandy to each and every one of the City young lads to ensure his favourite tipple was carried legally through customs.

It's fair to say there was one O'Neill I didn't get on with at Leicester City – John's Mrs. She was none too happy about someone coming to challenge her husband for a place in the City defence, particularly as he was only on week-by-week terms. The move also got me off to a frosty start with the Leicester Mercury's City reporter Bill Anderson, who was very friendly with O'Neill and rated him as a defender. I'm glad to say that particular relationship improved over the years. To be fair, Bill and the City lads were probably influenced by the fact I came to Filbert Street with a hard man reputation. They must have thought I was a hot headed youngster likely to pile up penalty points rather than points for winning football matches. I had to knuckle down, work hard and prove the doubters I was the genuine article. During the pre-season tour of Sweden and Germany, I struck up a particular friendship with Paul Ramsey, nicknamed Rambo by the fans but Penya to me. At first, Penya took a look at the new big man and had a go at me in training but soon realised we had plenty in common, not least the fact we were both top Grinders. Penya quickly accepted me and we became good friends.

I got the nod over O'Neill (sorry, Mrs O'Neill) for the opening league match of the season against Luton Town at Filbert Street, partnering Osman in central defence, in front of Ian Andrews between the sticks. Wasn't such a bad side altogether with Gary McAllister being one of our most outstanding players and dressers. I used to buy his cast off trousers and somehow fitted into them! Then there was Penya and Ali Mauchlen, also in midfield, and Mark Bright and Alan Smith up front. This was it: my first taste of the big time! I never slept that Friday night – and that was how it always was before a game for me. My task was to keep former Wigan team mate Mike Newell quiet - no easy task. Smith gave us the lead but the Hatters were the better side and a 1-1 draw was the very least they deserved. It was a good day for me though and Hamilton was well pleased.

I soon began to realise what a good player Russell Osman was. He starred for England and Ipswich and even played the part of a prisoner of war in the film *Escape to Victory*. To me, he was a class act in every way. A great guy to look up to, he took me under his wing in those early days. He had great feet and could ping the ball from one side of the pitch to the other. Russell was up there alongside Matt Elliott among the best defensive partners I ever played with. Os also gave me a few lessons in how to handle the hard stuff!

Victory over mighty Liverpool was a massive early boost for us and gave me an instant chance to play against two of my true football heroes. Although he was a completely different kind of defender, I always idolised Alan Hansen as a player. Even now, I can still see him striding into midfield with the ball at his feet. He was a player well suited to today's game. I was in closer contact, however, with the great Kenny Dalglish, the Reds' player manager. Somehow we managed to go 2-0 up before late on Dalglish took my breath away with a top drawer finish. I swear I had him covered but somehow he got himself a yard of space against me on the edge of the box and bent his shot into the top corner. All I could do was watch and admire it as it sailed into the net. Mind you, 2-1 was a fantastic win for us.

A 1-1 draw against Manchester United, when I marked Frank Stapleton out of the game, took us well up the early table before we gave our fans local bragging rights by coming back from behind at Filbert Street to beat fierce rivals Nottingham Forest 3-1. They were top of the table when they arrived in Leicester and we saw them off in style to move into ninth position ourselves. I remember thinking we were well set and I was really enjoying life in the top division. It couldn't get any better than this, could it? Sadly, the answer was no!

A week later I got my first Leicester red card in my unlucky 13th game for the Foxes at Charlton Athletic following a clash with former City striker Jim Melrose. We both went up for a genuine challenge and fell over. Melrose then had a spat at me and I lashed out in retaliation and caught him. I'm sure the referee knew of my reputation from Wigan as he had the card out before I made contact. I got a two-match ban, plus a club fine. Unbelievably, that was the start of a terrible run of 17 successive defeats away from Filbert Street.

A troubling groin injury finally took its toll when we went to Highfield Road to face Coventry City in the M69 derby. I'd been carrying it for a few games but felt it go completely in the warm up. Stupidly, I said nothing and played on. Competing against big Cyrille Regis on one leg wasn't easy but I had a really good first 45 minutes before admitting I couldn't come out for the second half. I had a fierce aerial battle with Regis and left my mark. See that egg-like lump on his forehead? That was me! We were beaten 1-0 by Cov as we slipped into the bottom three halfway through the campaign. Unfortunately that was my last real contribution of the season.

I never liked watching from the stands and seeing us slip further and further down the table as I struggled to get myself fit again made it even worse. There was a point when I felt fit enough to play but couldn't get back into the side. Frustration boiled over as I asked for a transfer, causing a rift in my usually good relationship with Bryan Hamilton. Looking back now, it was the rashness of youth; I was angry as I wanted to be in the side and stop our First Division life slipping away. I was also making a point. We were going through troubles at the top with Gordon Milne gone and Hamilton having problems dealing with the more forceful characters in the dressing room. A lot of players didn't get on with the boss and it was far from a happy camp. To be honest, he was dealt a very tough hand. Those City lads had been together for some time and formed cliques any new manager was going to struggle with.

Hamilton liked his long team meetings and took us to places like coal mines to see how the other half lived and what real hard labour was all about. I could see what he was getting at but it didn't make him popular with everyone. He also brought in a lot of new rules and handed out more than his fair share of fines. I'm not criticising Hamilton here because he was a good man but his headmaster-style wasn't working with many of the characters we had. On the other side of the coin, I was seen by the lads as a Hamilton man as I'd played for him at Wigan and that probably didn't do me too many favours settling into the club. Luckily, they soon realised I was a genuine northern lad and one of the boys who wouldn't always take the manager's side. I once walked into the dressing room to find my boots nailed to the floor, but that was Ali Mauchlen and the sense of humour of another great bloke I formed a fantastic relationship with on and off the field. Injured or not, I was fast becoming accepted as one of the lads.

A 1-1 draw against Wembley-bound Coventry City in the return game left our survival hopes hanging by a thread as we travelled to Oxford United for our final game. I sat nervously on the bench alongside Alan Smith knowing we needed to do better than Charlton Athletic to stay in the top league. Unfortunately we were held to a 0-0 draw and Charlton won. So, in my first season at Leicester City, I suffered the agony of being relegated and my First Division dream was in tatters.

A pre-season drinking incident in Sweden further undermined Hamilton's authority, in my view. High spirits were the norm with most clubs having a drinking culture in those days. I was involved but not the worst offender. Hamilton's threat to send us all home did nothing for our mood. That was only withdrawn after a particularly murderous training session.

Team bonding at Wigan was nothing compared with how we socialised at Leicester City. Like almost all clubs, we were barred from going out the night before a game. But if Friday was out, the evening before was fair game. So much so we called it the Thursday Club. Starting at Filbert Street's Captain Club bar, a lot of the players met after training to get things moving and it wasn't unusual for me to sink about nine or ten pints before driving home. Keeping up with Ali Mauchlen, as good a drinker as a player, was far from easy, but helped me overcome my early shyness and become part of the in-crowd at City. Ian Wilson was also there along with Paul Cooper. Altogether we were a great drinking squad. Steve Moran, who joined us from Southampton, was number one; he'd guzzle anything in large volumes. My image is of him holding a pint of Stella in both hands – one would be topped up whilst he drank the other. A lover of red wine and food, Moran had a great capacity for handling his booze and would usually shake it off with a good day's training on the Friday and be raring to go at the weekend. I say usually because once, he was so pissed, he accidentally ran into the guy mowing the pitch!

Walshy on Filbo: "Filbert Street was where I played all my football with City. The King Power is a great stadium but a lot of you will know what I mean when I say, had it been up to me, we'd never have left Filbo. Like most 'smallish' grounds, Filbo had a great atmosphere which we used to our advantage. I wasn't good at winning the toss but opposition skippers often played into our hands by allowing us to attack the Kop second half. Every time I won it you knew which way we would be kicking. I scored many a goal at both ends but nothing was like the feeling of scoring in front of the Kop. It was like sex but a million times better, as you know!

"When I think of Filbo, I can see the 20 or 30 lads perched on the Bentleys Roof – that always made me smile. Then there was the East Stand where we kicked balls over and had to rely on volunteers to try and get them back. I can still see that red card for smashing David Geddis and relive the tunnel scraps with too many players to mention.

"I enjoyed the small gym in the main stand where we played head tennis and characters who worked there including Sheila, in the laundry room, who was there before I joined and is still at City today. She's seen so many players and officials come and go. I still buy her a box of Black Magic chocolates for Christmas. I also remember Stan and Mary Brown in the old players' lounge and groundsman Steve repairing the divots and good old kit man Taff and his wife Rita Davies.

"The pitch suffered because of the shadow of the Double Decker stand meaning it was often a quagmire, either a foot deep in iced water or covered in a ton of sand. Our feet sank so deep our boots had to have big studs in wet conditions.

I remember a bird I used to 'larrup' whilst I was injured. I got on my bike, stopped for a big breakfast first, then did the business and took a shortcut back to the training ground with a smile on my face. Happy days those!

"We had the balloon cover to try to get matches on in bad weather and Bryan Hamilton, in particular, regularly called in fans to help shift the snow while other matches were off.

"All that is left of old Filbo today is the car park and fantastic memories – I still drive in there sometimes and think what used to be. I always tell the children on stadium tours 'over there is Filbert Street, where we used to play' ......fucking great, eh?"

I couldn't have made a worse start to life in Division Two. A horror incident with Shrewsbury Town's David Geddis produced a seemingly never-ending ban and could easily have ended my City career. We clashed several times during the game with the big striker elbowing me three times – my mood not being helped when referee Philip Don laughed at me after the final incident. That said, there was absolutely no excuse for what happened when Geddis scored the winning goal. My only explanation is that, as happened quite often, the red mist came down and I totally lost control. I smashed him with my elbow shattering his jaw in three places. Some of his teeth fell out and he was out of the game for 10 weeks. Don didn't need to send me off - I walked before he got his card out in the 89th minute and left to face the music. I got an automatic two-match ban but much worse was in store a few weeks later when the FA called me to a special disciplinary hearing at Lancaster Gate after reading the referee's report. That meant another six matches on top. Geddis took out a private prosecution against me and I received a heavy fine I couldn't afford - but the lads all weighed in to help. Goodness knows what would have happened had the incident taken place under the microscope of today's almost blanket TV coverage. That would have increased the pressure on City to kick me out. As it was, the press went to town but the club – and Hamilton in particular – gave me great support. Looking back, I owe them even more than I realised for giving me another chance.

Events snowballed fast. Opponents knew the pressure I was under and stuck the boot in. Whilst appealing the six-match ban, I mistimed an innocuous tackle on Ron Futcher who went down rather theatrically. To be fair, the striker spoke out on my behalf afterwards but the damage was done – and I'm not talking about Bradford City's 2-0 victory. That yellow card took me over the 20 point limit and meant, far from reducing my ban, I had it extended by another three! That was 11 matches in total – bloody hell, that was even a record for me!

On the plus side, I scored my first ever goal for the Foxes in a 3-0 victory over West Brom at Filbert Street in October and followed it up with another three days later in a 2-2 draw at Hull City. Hamilton, however, wasn't so lucky. Not only were we not promotion material but staying in the Second Division was becoming a fight.

Players were a lot to blame, in my view, for not giving their all for a boss some had fallen out with and made his sacking almost inevitable. So in came David Pleat in January 1988.Things soon began to look up both on and off the field with improved results and my first son Nicholas bouncing into the world in March. I was voted City's Player of the Season for the first time in just my second season and was also second leading goalscorer with seven in the league. Only midfielder Gary McAllister beat me in what was a more than disappointing campaign for our strikers. In other words, they were crap.

Talk was in the air that consolidation under Pleat was just the start and we'd be heading for a promotion challenge come August. But I was never far from trouble as an incident in a nightclub in Scotland on a pre season tour ended with a broken hand. Trouble brewed when Tony Spearing sprayed beer on the dancers from the balcony. One of the locals headed up the stairs to confront Tony and smacked an innocent Peter Weir. We all raced up to help out and got thrown down the stairs and out into the street where the action really started. Peter Weir, holding his eye and telling the bloke it wasn't him, nearly took another until I stepped in and smacked him. As the same man came towards me again, he got the left I knew I possessed bang smack on the button and went down. I held his throat and gave him another for good measure. But he moved his head and I hit the tarmac breaking my hand. It all kicked off after that with Ali Mauchlen steaming in only to injure his foot. Another guy started to give it all the martial arts moves but then shit himself and ran off - end of story. All three of us headed back to the hotel and you should have seen breakfast: there was Ali with his foot, Weir's big black eye and I couldn't hold a spoon as my hand was so swollen. We had to think quick before training and the game that evening, so all of us stayed out of the way of Gordon Lee who was in charge. When training started, first Peter Weir collided with an elbow - allegedly - then Ali miskicked someone's boot before I fell over rolling around holding my hand. Lee immediately sent me to the hospital from where I came back in a plaster cast. How we covered up that one was unreal. None of us were fit for the game and, worse still, when we arrived at the ground we saw the injured bloke we'd messed up seeking revenge. That was one rare night when I kept a low profile!

The expected good start didn't happen and 1988-1989 proved another frustrating season as I struggled with a groin injury. One of my few memories was a battle on and off the field with Noel Blake at Elland Road. I don't know what wound him up but he spent the whole 90 minutes trying to get me. I had a very good game but almost threw it all away a couple of minutes from time when I handled the ball only for penalty king Paul Cooper to save the spot kick and earn us a 1-1 draw. I hobbled off before half time then played throughout the second half in agony. I still have no idea what I did to upset Blake but we were still arguing when we left the pitch and there was almost a full scale fight in the players' bar afterwards. He came over to me giving it the big one but didn't realise I had my ex para mate next to me fist clenched. I told him to do one and the whole place nearly went up. Luckily, doormen intervened.

I was in the side for a couple of tasty local derbies against Forest in the League Cup. We just failed to make our advantage count after Stuart Pearce was sent off in the first half of a 0-0 Filbert Street draw before going out 2-1 at the City Ground in the replay.

Walshy on Stuart Pearce: "Psycho was one of football's genuine hard men and a crunching tackle between me and him would have been tasty. But my biggest collision with the former England captain came completely out of the blue. Millsy and I used to meet at the Durham Ox off the A46 where one of us would leave our car and the other would drive to training. I was in the driving seat coming home from Leicester when I pulled off the A46 and straight into an oncoming vehicle. It was totally my fault; I was ready to hold my hands up for a rank bad piece of driving. Who walked out of the other car but Stuart Pearce! I thought this was my worst nightmare. "Walshy, what the fuck are you doing?" he growled. Then he laughed at the unlikeliness of the situation even though his vehicle came off far worse in the accident and refused my offer to pay for the damage. Phew, what a top man!"

The following season of 1989/90 again saw us fail to get above mid table despite Pleat bringing in good players such as young Arsenal striker Kevin Campbell and Paul Moran from Spurs on loan. It was also round one of my famous long running feud with Wolves striker Steve Bull at Filbert Street in November. Perhaps one of the reasons we clashed so fiercely was because of our similarities. I was City through and through and prepared to die for our cause and Bully was exactly the same about Wolves. It was the irresistible force against the unmoveable object - someone, had to give. With England officials watching, Bully lost it as he struck out at me and saw red just before half time. Got to admit that was my first ever dive, but it worked. The game finished 0-0.

Campbell was one of the best young prospects in the country and a great guy in the dressing room. He was on target in an unbelievable match at Newcastle in January. The Geordies were on a winless run but got themselves in front early on before Tommy Wright equalised and I took advantage of goalkeeper John Burridge's fumble to hook us 2-1 in front. It was all square again before the break but we seemed to be in full control afterwards as Gary McAllister smashed in a screamer and Campbell supplied a cool finish to give us a 4-2 lead with time running out. But we conceded a soft goal soon afterwards and, with the home fans roaring them on, knew we were in a battle. When the score got to 4-4, we would have taken a point only for Mark McGhee , of all people, to pop up with a late winner for Newcastle.

I was fit and raring to go for 1990/91. But there was no change in my fortunes on the pitch as I was sent off in a 6-0 drubbing at Middlesbrough. This was just after the last man rule came in and I was dismissed in the 38th minute, sparking a three-goal rush from Boro that had the hordes of City fans crying in the Ayresome Park rain by half time. I heard each goal go in and felt I'd let my team mates down badly. We were absolutely shocking away from home, as that was our fifth successive defeat with 16 goals being shipped. To make it worse, I then ruptured ligaments in my right ankle in November and faced a long lay-off.

Again I fought my way back only to shoot myself in the foot in an FA Cup tie at Millwall. There was no excuse for my latest violent behaviour; it was caused entirely by frustration. We were winning the tie 1-0 and looking comfortable when my mate Paul Ramsey swung an arm towards the end and got himself sent off. The Lions then roared back with two goals, including one from Teddy Sheringham, to turn the game round and leave us staring at an early exit. In the last minute I jumped, studs showing, into Millwall goalkeeper Kasey Keller and we finished the game with nine men. It was a long walk off and, as I came down the mesh tunnel, hundreds of Lions fans spat all over me as I laughed in their faces. Pleat went crazy at Ramsey and I in the dressing room and the trip home was a silent one.

Matters came to a head at the end of January when we were losing 3-1 at home to Blackburn and a pitch invasion by unhappy City fans protesting against Pleat and the board was followed two days later by the resignations of both the manager and chairman Terry Shipman. I liked Terry and his lovely family, including wife Renee and daughter Maxine and her now husband Peter Kerr, both of whom I am still big friends with. Terry was very kind to me and I'll always be grateful to him for signing me. He sadly passed away a few years ago after a long illness and, tragically, his wife died soon afterwards in a car accident.

Pleat was a very interesting guy to work for. The first thing I must say is that he was always good to me and I thank him very much for that. There's no doubt he's very intelligent and, when I listen to him as a football pundit, he always talks a very good game. But communicating those ideas to footballers playing at below the highest level was far more difficult. He wanted us to play perfect passing football, which was fair enough, and I learned a lot from him. He urged me to use the ball better and, thanks to him, I started to see angles and positions I'd never looked for previously. But he got the balance wrong between skill and the physical side, in my opinion. We were still in days when there were fierce tackles, both foul and fair, and Pleat's City team was too nice and lightweight to win its battles. I saw much the same thing when he managed Tottenham Hotspur, a side full of talent but too easily beaten when the going got tough.

To his credit, he tried everything he knew to get the team moving in the right direction including introducing us to a few things that were completely new. He took us down to Henlow Grange, near Luton, a health spa, at the kind invitation of Stephen Purdew, a great guy who still looks after me with regular stays at Champneys. Three or four times a season we would go there to try to get in the right mental and physical shape for the challenges we faced on the field. Usually, the whole first team squad enjoyed an overnight stay to get together, relax and bond. Treatments such as massages and facials were fair enough but the yoga in which we were laid out on a mat led to one hilarious incident. The female instructor told us to relax, which the manager clearly took to heart. For when the rest of us got up off the floor, there was Pleat fast asleep snoring his head off!

It was there that we met boxer and TV personality Frank Bruno, then at the height of his powers and fame, training for a big fight. I found him to be a very friendly and likeable bloke with that laugh of his and a very genuine nature.

Pleat's ideas would probably be better accepted these days now sports science has changed the way footballers prepare for games. There's no doubt what you eat and drink and your state of mind is very important when you go out and compete. But one or two things were pure bollocks such as when the manager brought in an instructor to help us maintain our posture as we got off the gym equipment. I think, on occasions, Pleat looked too deeply into things instead of keeping it simple.

Where good psychology would have helped was when individuals were having a bad time on the pitch. There was very little help on offer back then if you were feeling down. It was largely down to you to pull yourself together and very easy to get into a rut. Make a mistake, lose a bit of confidence and the cycle went on. In contrast, as I know from the courses I've attended, the Football Association is doing a great job today in attending to such needs. They train coaches to look out for signs a player is struggling mentally and how to encourage and motivate – all part of a fast changing sport.

Pleat played strange mind games, explaining that we needed to keep alert and think for every second of 90 minutes. Typically we'd be training in the D of the penalty box jogging on the spot when the gaffer came up behind us and asked a general knowledge question. I went down in his estimation when I said the capital of Sweden was Oslo! Mind you, that wasn't as bad as Alan Paris who didn't know whether a tomato was a fruit or a vegetable. Another oddity was when Pleat suddenly produced a pink hair brush from his pocket to comb his quiff whilst talking with us.

City made a very sensible decision when Pleaty was sacked by promoting Gordon Lee from his coaching role to take over as caretaker manager. Gordon managed at the top level with Newcastle United, Blackburn Rovers and Everton and was well respected at the club. It was good to work under him, even if only for a few weeks. Ally, a big voice in the dressing room, was made player/coach.

I came back from suspension to help us to a 2-1 win against Barnsley but brief breathing space was lost as we suffered four successive defeats to fall back into the relegation zone. Even the good days were bad as we fought against dropping into the Third Division. We had a terrific 2-0 victory against Notts County at Meadow Lane but I was sent off and suffered a broken nose for my troubles. Big County striker Dave Regis swung his elbow from a throw in flush on my bugle. The fact he was the main sinner was no consolation for me seeing red for the third time that season.

We couldn't find any consistency and a couple more defeats meant our fate boiled down to an unbelievable last day. We needed to better West Bromwich Albion's result in our home game against Oxford United or the unthinkable would really happen. We'd been up and down from the top two divisions like a yo-yo but City fans were proud we had never been any lower. I went into the game having had the major boost a few weeks earlier of the birth of my second son, Matthew, on a night that was crazy to say the least. I took a phone call at a sportsman's dinner and tried to drive home as fast as I could – fuck the speed limit. The result was a very untimely blue light and a breathalyser test which proved negative. Again my reputation didn't help as police demanded another test before accepting my story. That was also clear and I eventually got back to Debbie with three penalty points on my licence.

Saturday, May 11, 1991 was probably one of the tensest days in the club's history. We didn't want to let our proud fans down. People say the nervous tension is far different depending on whether you are going for promotion or trying to avoid the drop – and they're spot on. It's exciting battling away near the top of the table; anticipation is also in the air when you're in trouble but it's a feeling of dread in the pit of your stomach. Everyone is shitting it and doesn't want to make mistakes. It's even worse when your destiny isn't entirely in your own hands as we needed West Brom to drop points against Bristol Rovers at Twerton Park. Nowadays, every second person in the crowd knows exactly what is happening at crucial games affecting their team, but that wasn't the case back then. With some fans having transistor radios, all sorts of rumours used to be passed on as fact. It was said that Rovers were down to ten men and West Brom had missed two penalties. Neither was true. Worse still at half time, we were officially told Rovers were winning 2-0 when it was only one.

If ever I saw proof of the loyalty of Leicester City fans it was that tense Saturday. Our average gate was less than 12,000 - understandable considering how we were playing – but there was a full house against Oxford. The huge crowd was one reason why we came out of the traps quickly and put Oxford under early pressure. Our perilous plight was made for characters with heart and commitment to the blue shirt and it was popular defender Tony James who wrote himself into City folklore by scoring what turned out to be the only goal after 24 minutes. It was a great moment for Tony made slightly strange by the fact most of the lads congratulated David Kelly. Tony told me afterwards that it was only when I said 'great goal' he fully believed it himself. If Tony hadn't netted, I was right behind him and would have scored. That should have been the first of many. We had enough play and chances to have won by six or seven but the ball just wouldn't go in. The second half lasted all weekend. Nothing too dramatic happened but knowing one small slip could change everything racked up the tension more and more. I constantly pushed us up to the halfway line making it difficult for the visitors to get out of their own half. Even Oxford getting their first and only corner towards the end seemed a major crisis.

Skipper Ali Mauchlen kept rallying the troops, however, and we made it through to the final whistle. Ali was as tough as it gets on a football field and could certainly dig. I remember him standing on Robin van der Laan's head in one tussle against Port Vale and that man was no pushover. Ali was a character you would want next to you in the trenches and just the kind we needed when our future was on the line.

Winning the match was no cause for celebration until we heard the 'real' final score from Twerton Park. 'Bristol Rovers one' came as a shock, but 'West Bromwich Albion one' was greeted like we'd won the Football League and European Cup all at once. It really was that important to us and the Leicester Mercury brought out a special supplement to celebrate our great escape.

Walshy on his strangest injury: "I was grateful for a lot of the medical attention I received during my career but not all my 25 operations were necessary.

"Throughout my career, I suffered from numbness in my feet, usually in the first half. Many times I went down on the pitch for treatment because I couldn't feel my feet or anything from the knee down. I'd take my boots off during the interval and usually be a lot more comfortable in the second half – how weird! Surgeon Mike Allen diagnosed me with a version of carpal tunnel syndrome, more common in older people's wrists, and operated on both ankles. As soon as I got back onto the pitch, however, it made no difference at all – I still had the same lack of feeling.

"I also had the joy of having eight needles inserted into both calves by Allen while running on a tread machine to check whether it was a problem with blood circulation. But again there seemed to be no end to my problem.

"In the end, I diagnosed myself. The real cause of my problems for years and years was that I tied my boots too tight! It wasn't helped by my habit of having a red hot bath on a Friday night to mould the boots to my feet. As soon as I loosened up, I never had the same problem again."

Chapter Five

Little's Grinders and a 'Marked' Man

"
I can still see myself reeling away
to the corner flag and our fans going mental
"

APPOINTING Walshy as captain wasn't difficult: I gave him the job of being our leader on the pitch and he was just that. He was a commanding figure who never hid and always put himself on the line for the team. Whether he was having a good game or not, he'd always go flat out. Walshy handled the task of being the link between the manager and the rest of the lads very well. He never complained whatever I asked and our communication was spot on.

When I think about Walshy, I bracket him with Gary Mills; they were two completely different characters, but bounced off each other and both loved Leicester City Football Club. When I needed to alter things a little on the pitch and that involved Walshy, I'd call in Millsy alongside him and we'd sort things out.

I decided to play Walshy as part of a central back three, alongside the likes of Tony James and Richard Smith. That forced our opponents to cross the ball from deeper areas and suited Walshy who was particularly good in the air. He'd always play up front in our five and six-a-side training games and I put him up there to give him a breather from his responsibilities at the back. Walshy had his disciplinary problems on the field and was probably sent off and booked a few more times than he should have been during my time at Filbert Street. His short fuse was one of his traits as a player; sometimes it worked for us, sometimes against. There are very few people however who would say Walshy is anything other than a decent bloke.

BRIAN LITTLE, Leicester City manager 1991-94

CHEATING the dreaded drop opened the way to yet another new era for me at Filbert Street – one that led annually to Wembley, a life-changing match against local rivals Derby County and an all-too-brief spell in the Premier League.

New chairman Martin George swooped to bring in former Aston Villa and England striker Brian Little as our new manager. Like O'Neill when he arrived, Little served his time in the lower leagues, having done a great job with Darlington – and brought in former playing colleagues as part of his coaching team in Alan Evans, John Gregory, Steve Hunt as well as former Foxes legend David Nish. He booted out players he regarded as troublemakers but gave me a great vote of confidence.

Being made captain of Leicester City meant absolutely everything. In those days, I wore white tape around my arm as we didn't have armbands. Being in charge of the lads felt to me like being a chief officer in the army. To his credit, Little saw through my bad boy reputation and could see a good player who loved the football club. No doubt he was banking on extra responsibility giving me the incentive to get my discipline in order. The new manager said when he took the job that he had a three-year plan to take City into the Premier League – what a statement! He was bang on the button.

Little's was the best training regime I'd experienced to date and morale quickly improved. I backed the boss when he sold one of our best players Paul Kitson to Derby in exchange for Phil Gee and Ian Ormondroyd. It was a difficult one but contract talks had broken down with Kitson and a transfer was the best option. 'Sticks' was always going to be a handful with his height and scored a fair few with his feet, too, but I will always remember him for a very different near miss. He was clay pigeon shooting with Richard Smith, David Lowe and I in Norway on a pre-season tour. We were given strict instructions what to do with the guns but Sticks was in no mood to play by the rules. He pointed the gun as a joke at David Lowe before pretending to shoot. The instructor went ballistic but that wasn't going to spoil the striker's fun. A few minutes later it was his turn to try to shoot the pigeon but the gun didn't fire so he turned it downwards and the gun went off nearly blowing his feet off. He went white and the instructor banned him, taking his gun and calling him a 'crazy fucker'. I guess it was serious as I might not have scored my winning goal against the 'sheepshaggers' had Sticks lost his feet.

Man management was Little's strength. Sometimes a manager has to do the unexpected to get his message across and he was good at that. Called into training on the Monday morning after one defeat, we expected to be put through our paces. John Gregory, always great with the lads, had his bootlaces tied around his white socks to pose and told us to get on the team bus with trainers only. We thought we were going running at Bradgate Park but he took us to McDonalds for breakfast and it worked a treat.

Little was also strong and big enough to put up with my quirks. It's true I was terrible at changing my mind over our pre-match meals. I looked at the menu and made my choice like everyone else. Then when the food started to arrive, I'd fancy someone else's, not mine – that's food, not girlfriends, by the way! Instead of getting angry, the manager humoured me. Apparently, even when he was at Aston Villa, he'd see food and say "Walshy would like that!" That was just one way he saw the bigger picture – keeping me happy and in the best frame of mind to go on the pitch was more important to Leicester City than telling me to sort myself out.

I was often put forward to speak with the local media and particularly the Mercury's Bill Anderson, who was part of the City furniture for many years. Whereas you only see national journalists every now and again, it's different with locals, with whom you can build up a mutual trust. He needed us for a Leicester City story most days of the week and we saw him as the middle man between us and the fans.

To be honest, I probably became more cautious with reporters as my career progressed rather than the other way round. Problem was they were always looking for angles – and quite skilled at nudging me towards what they wanted me to say rather than what I really thought. I also found it confusing, at first, when chatting to journalists I knew after a match and not appreciating that everything I said was 'on the record'. This was particularly so when they weren't using recording devices and merely taking an odd note. I did get quoted wrongly or out of context on a number of occasions and was then brought to account by the manager, including Martin O'Neill, who banned us from speaking to the media completely at one stage. I think this is why we hear so many bland interviews from footballers these days as they are trained to fend off questions and not risk getting caught up in any controversy.

A Scotsman, who was a Hearts fan, Bill Anderson travelled with us even on our pre-season tours and I do have a confession here. He liked to read a book to pass the time and on one of our trips to Sweden I waited until he'd almost finished before secretly ripping the last few pages out. He went absolutely mental when he found out and was so wound up there was no way I was going to admit it. We also went out Kayaking and Millsy and I made him capsize in the icy waters of a forge in Trondeim, Norway. Again he survived – fortunately not to write the story!

We may not have been noticeably more talented than Pleat's side but, under Little, we learned how to grind out a result. Surviving a second half battering from Derby at the intimidating Baseball Ground to hold on for a 2-1 victory was a sign we were beginning to turn the corner. Happily for me, I was one of the City lads on the scoresheet in what was almost an East Midlands 'Old Firm' match for us.

Even more promising was holding our own against top flight opposition, a trend set early on that season when I equalised in the last minute to earn us a 1-1 draw against First Division champions Arsenal in the Rumbelows Cup. That was a big night for me in many ways as I had my first 'battle' with Ian Wright playing up front for the Gunners alongside our former loanee Kevin Campbell. Wrighty got the opening goal but then came my great moment. I outjumped those giants Steve Bould and Tony Adams to net a thunderous header that ensured we finished with honours even and a replay. We should have won as David Kelly had a goal disallowed for offside. No way, ref!

Later we knocked Crystal Palace out of the FA Cup when Bobby Davison got the winning goal against ten men in injury time and had a great run in the Zenith Data Systems Cup. In an early round, I helped us see off a storming Barnsley comeback at Filbert Street. We were three goals up early on before the Yorkshire side rallied to 3-3 and I scored the winner in extra time. But even that was nothing compared with a great win over First Division Notts County at Meadow Lane. We were a goal down and on the receiving end for most of the evening before Tommy Wright equalised towards the end of normal time and Paul Fitzpatrick grabbed the winner. I will never forget the several thousand Leicester fans behind that goal; what an adrenalin rush that gave me especially when I nutted Craig Short right in front of them and got away with it!

That left City officials licking their lips at the thought of a £100,000-plus pay day from the two legged semi final against old rivals Nottingham Forest. All the players were interested in though was the chance to put one over Brian Clough and earn a surprise day out at Wembley.

I didn't have too many dealings with 'Old Big Head' but those nights gave me a fair idea of the man in his last few years in the game. The first match was played in front of our own fans at Filbert Street on a Tuesday night. In those days one of my roles as City skipper was to report to the referee's room to hand over our team sheet. First to greet me was Cloughie, almost certainly the worst for wear, who kicked me hard down the front of my shin and said "I've heard you don't like being kicked, young man." I replied "Brian, you know I like being kicked!" Then he kicked me again, twice as hard before saying "I heard you don't like it!" Again I said "Brian, you know I do." Then he lent against the wall giving the referee a few choice words. Only Cloughie could get away with that kind of thing. Forest skipper Stuart Pearce just looked on in disbelief.

The match finished 1-1 and we were in the players' lounge afterwards when Pearce came over and apologised for Cloughie's actions. He told me after the game the manager asked him "Stuart, when are we in next?" and he'd answered "Friday, boss, for five-a-side", therefore giving himself and the rest of the players a couple of days off. Cloughie agreed. That was Cloughie's unusual way of doing things at the City Ground.

I was careful to keep out of kicking distance when we went to Nottingham for the return and the early signs were good. The handover of the team sheets passed without incident and when Cloughie, dressed more smartly than usual, marched beyond our players in the tunnel I thought we were all in the clear. Amazingly, he retraced his steps and went along the line of the whole City team, starting with me, clipping us all round the back of our heads in a gesture clearly meant to intimidate. That didn't worry me too much but it wasn't the best of nights for us as we went down 2-0, ending our Wembley hopes. To make things worse, Paul Reid was sent off.

Walshy on Cloughie: "One unforgettable incident was a referees' meeting at Filbert Street. I was sitting with Gary Mills and Cloughie was with his driver. The meeting had been going on for about an hour when Cloughie suddenly stood up and announced he had to be off because he was going shopping with his wife Barbara. He then said referees had got a hard job but were 'a fucking disgrace' – and walked out. Millsy and I were in bits laughing.

Our task after the cup exit was to get ourselves promoted so we could earn another couple of cracks at Forest the following season. We were in contention for an automatic slot almost all the way through only for a 2-0 defeat against Charlton, ground sharing at Upton Park, in our last but one match to leave us with just an outside chance on the final day. We had to beat Kevin Keegan's struggling Newcastle, who were in real danger of going down to the Third Division.

That would be enough to sneak the second automatic promotion spot if Middlesbrough failed to win at Wolves. It proved yet another emotional last day but without a happy ending – and gave an unwanted place for me in Newcastle folklore.

Our chances looked bleak when Newcastle's leading scorer Gavin Peacock took advantage of a mistake by Steve Thompson to delight their 2,000 travelling fans with a 1-0 interval lead. There were chances for both sides after the break as tension mounted but the main drama was reserved for the last few minutes with me at the centre of it all. My far post header hit the roof of the Newcastle net to level the scores and give us one last chance to get the winner. Instead, deep into injury time, Newcastle's goalkeeper smashed a long clearance downfield which I misjudged – a fatal mistake of letting the ball bounce. Turning backwards and, unaware Carl Muggleton was racing out of goal, I instinctively tried to stab the ball back to him but instead watched in agony as it dribbled slowly into the net. One of our spectators behind the goal came closer to saving it than Muggleton as fans of both sides then spilled onto the pitch. I remember my good mate Wayne North consoling me, then trying to nick my shirt off me. Referee David Elleray decided enough was enough and blew the final whistle – the best idea in what could have become very ugly circumstances. But I never heard Elleray's whistle go and waited for several minutes for the game to resume by which time I was surrounded by fans from both sides. I had to be told by a fan that the game was over before leaving the field in dejection.

It was an unforgettable afternoon but didn't affect the outcomes at either end of the table as it turned out. Boro won 2-1 to book their place in the top flight and results at the bottom meant Newcastle would have survived even if they lost. But try telling that to the fans and players who went through an emotionally draining afternoon.

Defeat meant we slipped down a place below Derby to fourth and were handed the very physical challenge of John Beck's Cambridge United in the play off semi final to try to book a place at Wembley. The first leg at the Abbey Stadium wasn't for the faint hearted as I had a massive battle with Dion Dublin. It started in the very first minute when Dublin nearly broke my leg with a late high tackle. I hold my hands up and admit I laid him out with an elbow in the second half completely off the ball – but he landed enough blows of his own that night. That was just one occasion when I was very relieved the referee wasn't on top of his job. Had he seen the incident properly and shown me a red card, I'd have been automatically suspended for Wembley and rightly so.

As for the football itself 'The Rooster' Kevin Russell added to his popularity with the Foxes fans by giving us the lead but we ended well satisfied with a 1-1 draw after coming under pressure after the home side equalised. You almost knew we would do them in the return at fortress Filbo!

We expected a tough game and that seemed likely when Cambridge came at us strongly from the kick off. But this was one of those rare matches when pretty much everything went right for us. Tommy Wright and Steve Thompson put us 2-0 up at half time and we destroyed them afterwards with a three-goal blitz in five golden minutes – Rooster, Wrighty and Ian 'Sticks' Ormondroyd doing the demolition job. A first Wembley final for 23 years was magnificent consolation after a dramatic season but there was only one thing on my mind: we had to beat Blackburn Rovers. That was no mean feat against a side managed by Liverpool legend Kenny Dalglish and owned by mega rich Jack Walker.

There can't be a game anywhere as tense as the play-off final for a place in what is now the Premier League. The money stakes have been cranked up since our epic battles, of course, but the same familiar pressure was there. Having worked so hard for more than nine months, everything depended on just 90 minutes of football. Brian decided to take us down to Wembley two days earlier to watch the Third and Fourth Division play-off finals in a bid to allow lads, who had never experienced the national stadium before, to get acclimatised. Instead it probably prolonged the agony – all that waiting around made us more nervous, I think.

The Blue Army were fantastic, as always, on a red hot day. An amazing 38,000 travelled to support us as temperatures edged into three figures inside the stadium. Leading Leicester City out at Wembley for the first time was a tremendous honour, I looked around the stadium as I proudly walked the team out; it was a sea of blue and white, the atmosphere was electric and the national anthem made me very emotional. You had to be there to understand, but once again, as against Manchester City in the FA Cup Final all those years before, we were on the wrong end of a narrow 1-0 scoreline.

I think every true Fox left Wembley cursing David Speedie for his part in that goal. But I was in the best position of all to judge that terrible penalty after referee George Courtney, taking charge of his last ever match, gave the decision against me. I put my arm across the Scottish forward admittedly and I swear he meant to push the ball down my left side. Instead he miskicked it and it ended up squirting between my legs. Speedie then dived forward and hit the deck. I'm honest enough to admit I was guilty of obstruction but Speedie's gamesmanship won the day. We could argue about it forever, but I'm not going to start the war up again here. Had Speedie won that penalty for us during his spell at Filbert Street, none of us would have complained. We'd have slapped him on the back and congratulated him. I always call him a cheat when I see him but it's all forgiven now – just never forgotten. Former City striker Mike Newell stuck the spot kick away in the last minute of the first half. As I walked back to the changing rooms even Dalglish looked at me and said it was harsh. We had our chances to put things right with efforts from Simon Grayson and Sticks whacked off the line with their goalkeeper beaten as we piled on the pressure before our goalkeeper Carl Muggleton, who also had a great game, saved a second Newell penalty at the death.

I admitted it at the time – and again now – the pressure got to me during those final weeks of the season. I was haunted by the Newcastle own goal and on a knife-edge after the Cambridge game worried sick the Dublin incident would rule me out of Wembley. The fact it was my first time with City at Wembley and I was a letdown, allowing Speedie to destroy our season, killed me. It's strange how things work out. Thanks to that controversial win, Rovers went on to become Premier League champions a couple of seasons later whilst we went through more nightmares before joining them.

Getting beaten by Blackburn was one thing, nearly getting killed on our close season visit to Spain was even worse! The scene was a familiar one: we were relaxing after a hard season and having a few drinks. When I say a few drinks, you know what I mean. My good mate Julian Joachim had me on these green Iguana cocktails with a nice combination of vodka and tequila. They slipped down well but even I was a bit out of my depth and I was very drunk. I decided to walk back to the hotel alone, but things nearly kicked off with a group of Germans having a pop at me. I told them what to do before a woman came screaming round the corner and left her sporty car bang in the middle of the road, engine running, right in front of me before rushing into a bar to start an argument with somebody. There are moments of madness and moments of real madness – this was one of the latter. For some reason, I thought it would be fun to jump into her car and have a drive as a joke. I didn't mean any harm; I was just having a laugh. I got to the end of the street - a dead end – then returned saluting the Germans out of the window - but when I say 'salute', you know what I mean! Suddenly six Spanish men pushed a wheelie bin into the road to block me and cut my joy ride short. As the door opened, I was booted in the face and dragged out of the car where I was attacked by seven blokes, one carrying a metal bar and another with a kosh. I was soon getting absolutely battered and in real trouble. My last resort was to try to play dead but, luckily, Smudger arrived and smashed three or four of them to set me free. In all honesty, I thank him for saving my life. Meanwhile Carl Muggleton sat on a wall, frozen with fear and unable to come and help me. We were then surrounded and Smudger fancied some more. I took the big guy out first with the bar and Smudger took the lad with the kosh, But we were again outnumbered. Suddenly the Spanish ran off as the police arrived and shoved us all in the back of their van, even Muggy, who had done nothing wrong, just melted!

What happened next made me laugh through the pain. I will never forget Smudger's face looking at me in stitches as the goalkeeper protested his innocence and we kept telling him to shut up. They banged us up for a few hours but were just worried whether I needed hospital treatment before finally letting us go. Brian Little didn't get to know the full details as he was staying with the coaching staff at the other side of the island but realised something was up when he came to see us all the next day and saw my lip which still carries the scars today. Truth was I wasn't bothered at all by my near death experience as long as that massive scab didn't scupper my good looks!

We all needed to start the 1992/93 season well to get the Wembley defeat out of our systems but I suffered the exact opposite. This was where my much-publicised feud with Wolves striker Steve Bull began making more headlines. The two of us have earned a few quid talking about our rivalry on the question and answer circuit in recent years and today it's all water under the bridge. There was no doubt about it, though, on the field we didn't get on at all. In our second match of the campaign at Wolves it was my turn. Bully fouled me three times in the first 15 minutes before he got a yellow – that's a hell of a lot of lip biting for a character like me! But it was my sheer frustration at making a mistake a few minutes later to let Bully in to score for Wolves that finally did it for me. I hit him hard from behind - a trademark Walsh Glasgow kiss – and down he went. Once I realised the referee had spotted it, I knew there was no escape. I was off and we lost 3-0. Bet you all remember my sorry long walk off past the empty stand to the portacabin dressing rooms. After 17 months of keeping out of trouble, prompting talk that I'd cured my discipline problem once and for all, I was back to square one. I was really gutted and depressed by what I'd done; I had cost the club points and myself another two weeks wages. Before that incident, Spurs offered £750,000 to take me to White Hart Lane. But a player who couldn't control himself on the field was not going to be much use to anyone, let alone a club of their magnitude.

WALSHY was similar to me – we were young and raw and like two
wild bulls coming together for a fight when we played against each other. I was
first to get sent off at Filbert Street in front of England manager Bobby Robson,
then it was Walshy's turn at Molineux. I clipped his heels on purpose and he got
back up, ran at me and head-butted me. Even then we'd have a bit of banter about
who had got who after the match. As Walshy says, we could have both seen red
several times and it was always a physical clash between us. Neither set out to
seriously hurt the other: I was doing all I could to score and he was doing the
same to stop me.

We came to respect each other more and more, partly because we were both
loyal to our clubs. Walshy was Leicester through and through and that's absolutely
brilliant. I know when you stop at one club how you can get to love the place. Got
to say that when he was playing alongside Matt Elliott, they were two of the best
defenders in the English game. They both looked 6'6" and there just didn't seem
a way past them. I'd have Walshy in my side every day of the week.

We've talked about our rivalry at many public events since and I consider Walshy
a mate. He's a top, top man and, if he needed something, I'd do anything I could.

STEVE BULL MBE, Wolves striker 1986-1999

Little spoke publicly of having seen a side of me he was very disappointed in and
warned I was going nowhere in my career unless I learned how to handle the big
occasions. He was right. But, with a young Julian Joachim beginning to make
an impression up front, we actually started the season very well and were up to
third place before the Charlton jinx struck again on Halloween. Yet another red
card - my seventh in a City shirt – followed a clash with another of my rivals, Carl
Leaburn. He was another guy who put himself about a bit and could be naughty
with it but I was a little unlucky. I got a yellow for an obstruction on Gary Nelson
when some claimed I used an elbow then a couple of minutes later the Charlton
players ganged up on me to get me sent off after Leaburn made the very most of
a foul. I sat dejected and furious with myself in the dressing room and decided to
phone my mate Andy Sattersthwaite to give me a lift home in his car even before
the final whistle, which I knew would have serious consequences. That was too
much for Little, who after being told by the chairman that he needed to take action,
stripped me of the captaincy and gave it to my close pal Gary Mills. I was also fined
two weeks wages. The money I could cope with but losing the captaincy was a huge
body blow as that meant everything to me. It was my badge of honour. But, as ever,

Little found a way of getting me back on the straight and narrow and gain a '£1m striker' into the bargain.

Little threw me up front when I returned from a four-match ban to keep me out of trouble. To be fair, I had no argument but still felt he could have done something else as a punishment and not strip me of the captaincy. He may have thought the burden of leading the line was too much for talented 19-year-old Julian Joachim. But even he must have been surprised at how well the switch worked. I experienced the role at professional level at Wigan but playing at centre half was also very useful. I'd seen enough of strikers at the closest of quarters to know the runs they make and the tools of the trade. I was always going to be a physical threat in the air and as brave as a lion, but I could also hold up the ball when I needed to and link up well with Jocky.

There's nothing better for your confidence in football than getting on a goalscoring run. Mine started with a goal against Swindon in a 4-2 win and continued against Watford, a 5-2 barnstormer at Filbert Street in which I played both up front and in defence at different stages. I netted eight in nine matches at one point and was up to 14 for the season. You can only imagine how much I enjoyed showing my old mate Leaburn how it should be done by scoring a couple in our 3-1 victory in the return game against Charlton. Lee Philpott banged over a couple of great crosses and I gave them the full treatment with two headers. There were a couple of sayings among Leicester fans I became aware of – 'Walshy for England' went a little too far but the other one made me very proud because it was true. It was a fact that, whenever I scored, City didn't lose, at least until we went to Newcastle!

The Charlton game was also notable for a second incident involving Leaburn in which he spat in my face. His card was now well and truly marked after his part in my sending off but the opportunity for revenge didn't come that day. Instead I got him back just when he wasn't expecting it during a later away game. I wasn't in the best of moods anyway as I trooped off at half time with us losing by a goal to nil and that was made no better by seeing Leaburn, who wasn't in the Charlton side, dressed in a smart suit . As I was walking down the tunnel, he took a quick look at me. I wasn't going to get a better chance than this. So I punched him to remind him not to mess with me again. There was a big melee in the tunnel before I got into our dressing room. Little was doing the team talk when there was a knock at the door. Two policemen wanted to speak to "the number five about an incident in the tunnel". They both escorted me arm in arm to the referee's room where they asked the official whether he had seen anything. Luckily, he hadn't. I was allowed back into our dressing room scot free with the manager understandably looking bewildered. So I escaped both the clutches of the referee and the law and played on during the second half. City lost the battle on the pitch, but Leaburn needed no reminding Walshy got his revenge. I was really pleased with myself. That was yet another red I escaped!

We could have done without having to go to champions Newcastle United on the last day of the regular league season. Keegan's men had celebrated their last gasp reprieve against us 12 months earlier by rampaging through the division with Andy Cole scoring goals for fun. Meanwhile we'd once again made the play offs whatever the result at St James Park. We never thought for a second the Geordies would take it easy but six nil at half time was a huge shock. Andy Cole helped himself to a hat trick with home fans singing his name. Strangely enough, I was having a good game, causing the home defence their fair share of problems as Little kept me up front. Then, in the second half, I put the ball into the back of the net for our goal in a 7-1 defeat – a little too late to save my record - and Newcastle supporters started singing my name! To be honest, it probably had more to do with my own goal 12 months earlier but it made me laugh during a match I'd otherwise prefer to forget.

That meant we finished sixth and were paired in the play off semi final with the side who had most reason to feel unlucky, third placed Portsmouth. They missed out on automatic promotion only on goal difference having got 12 more points than us. Did I feel any sympathy for them? In a way, yes. Like most football folk, I'm a big fan of the play offs and the fantastic drama they provide at the end of the season. But players know the league table doesn't lie over 46 games and it was harsh on Pompey to begin all over again on a level playing field. I'm not sure what the answer is but perhaps the third side should qualify for Wembley or, at least, have a one off home semi final as a reward for finishing higher.

On this occasion, however, Pompey weren't the only ones feeling a bit out of joint. We'd known for some time we'd have to play the 'home' leg on foreign soil as the Carling Stand was being built at Filbert Street. Being told that venue was Forest's City Ground brought mixed emotions. It wasn't a place where we'd got good results in recent years and, for Foxes fans in particular, the rivalry between City and Forest is the strongest of the lot. Whatever our private thoughts, we had to be professional and get on with it – and that's just what we did. A single goal from my mate Julian Joachim gave us a narrow lead to take to Fratton Park. I played up front in the first leg but Brian Little moved me back into defence for the expected Portsmouth onslaught in the midweek return. I couldn't prevent Pompey scoring a

Walsh v Keane collision time

No.1 striker Emile Heskey

NP and I hold up the Championship trophy

An expensive red card for Walshy at Chelsea – 40k

MOM Coca-Cola Cup winners 1997

Famous last gasp equaliser against Arsenal

Leading a golf day with TC

A painful defeat at Grimsby

Two-goal Stan the man

Never a penalty, referee! FA Cup pain at Chelsea

Gazza celebrates at my testimonial

Gazza entertains...

Walshy and Muzzy's soccer academy

Legend Muzzy

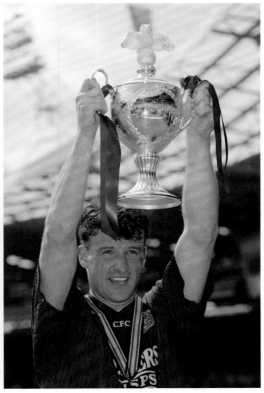

1986 First game v Manchester United

1994 Cup celebration

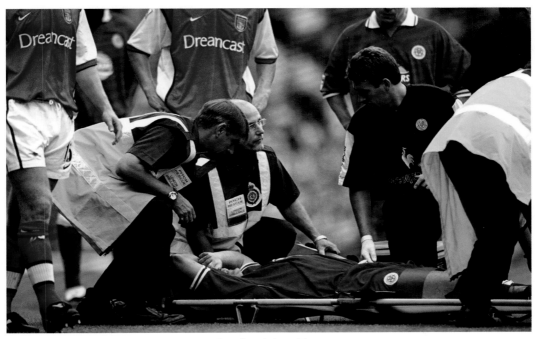

Another injury blow

The best decision I ever made

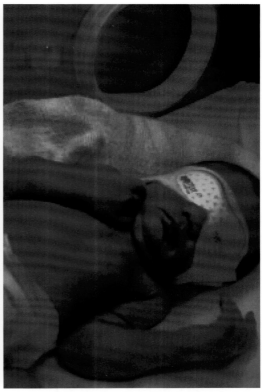

Two handsome gents – me and my dad

Premature Zaki struggles at LRI

The Walsh family charity match v Forest

Best Man Crampy

Me and my old-man

love our Sue, my sister

Me and the 'Tank Commander'

couple of goals but Ian Ormondroyd and Steve Thompson replied for us and we were through to Wembley yet again on a 3-2 aggregate.

The manager changed his Wembley schedule for the clash with Glenn Hoddle's Swindon Town by opting to train at Belvoir Drive and travel down to London the night before. After the Blackburn game, I felt he did the right thing - but still our luck was bang out. City fans reminded me over and over again just how incredible they were during those days when we almost made Wembley our second home. I remember pulling up to the big Wembley gates and then going out onto the pitch for our day of destiny to be confronted with a sea of blue and white. It was scary, believe me. Imagine 38,000 Leicester City fans desperate to roar us back into the top flight. But we ran into exactly the same problem that had plagued us against Blackburn – poor refereeing, I was no great fan of David Elleray, an official in the headmaster style, but that wouldn't have mattered had he got the key decisions right.

STEVE epitomises everything about Leicester's never-say-die attitude. When the odds were stacked against us, a goal down in the last few minutes it always seemed to be Walshy in some way that would push the rest of the team on to success.

He battled the opposition on the pitch, playing though injuries and never quitting despite many career threatening injuries that would have finished most other footballers.

To all Leicester fans including me, Walshy was and still is a huge inspiration and a real local hero

By Jim Sehmi, Leicester fan and director E L Group

We could have no complaints about Hoddle himself, still a fantastic player in the twilight of his career. The former England midfielder gave Swindon the lead just before half time with a low shot from the edge of the box but worse was to follow. A neat one-two saw Craig Maskell double our deficit two minutes after the break before the first of Elleray's major cock ups seemed to settle the tie. When the ball went behind our goal line almost everyone at Wembley could see it was a goal kick. Yet Elleray pointed to the corner and they scored a scrappy third through Shaun Taylor. I told Elleray exactly what I thought and, as usual, it did me no favours. The yellow card, however, was the least of my worries as we were 3-0 down with about 35 minutes to go and all but finished. Or that's how everyone else thought. In my mind, I wasn't going to let this happen. No way.

I tried everything to rally the troops and the turnaround was one of the most amazing I ever experienced in my football career. I'm not exaggerating when I say I almost singlehandedly got us back into that match by bullying our players into action. I vividly remember my far post header from Lee Philpott's cross. I rose above centre half Shaun Taylor and connected perfectly with a tremendous, powerful header. I thought it was in but, as I fell over, I heard it crash against the post. For the first time in the whole afternoon, our luck was in as the ball rebounded straight to Joachim who smashed home from six yards. Reducing the deficit to 3-1 gave the rest of the lads reason to believe we were back in it. We swarmed all over Swindon and the second goal came from weight of pressure more than anything else. It was one-way traffic now. The ball flashed across their goalmouth before Philpott retrieved possession near the byline. His high looping cross from the left was more central and I rose to beat goalkeeper Fraser Digby and head into the empty net. That was 3-2 and the fans were smelling Swindon blood. I definitely was!

Then came a moment of complete jubilation – a goal I will never forget as long as I live. Our equaliser with 20 minutes to go was unreal. Mike Whitlow made a great run down the left and played a clever pass back inside for Thommo who took the ball in his stride, rounded a defender and placed his shot just inside the post. I swear I have never had a feeling like it ever in my life – the whole of Wembley erupted, the finest comeback the famous ground had ever seen was on the cards. Surely at 3-3 this was going to be our day…Swindon were gone. They were on the ropes like a boxer waiting to be knocked out with one final punch.

We had the one great chance to lay them out shortly afterwards when David Oldfield over ran the ball inside the Swindon penalty area. The sheer physical effort to get ourselves back into the game was beginning to tell but that had nothing to do with the winning goal. Dashing out of his goal, Kevin Poole couldn't help but collide with Steve White who had lost the ball anyway. It was never a penalty but, for the second time in successive years, the one person who mattered ruled differently. Paul Bodin rolled the spot kick into the same corner in which Newell had shattered our dreams. How cruel can football be! To be honest, it was probably the worst I ever felt after a football match. I remember watching TV several days later - they played the song *Everybody Hurts* by REM to accompany pictures of our devastated players on the Wembley pitch after the final whistle. That image is still ingrained in my mind today.

Walshy on referees: I honestly believe many refs didn't want to see my name on the teamsheet. They knew they were in for a difficult day because I never gave them a moment's peace. I didn't often swear at officials but was always in their ear, letting them know exactly what I thought. One exception was when David Elleray awarded Swindon that decisive penalty in the play off final. I called him a 'cheating twat' because he'd cheated us out of the game in my opinion with that decision. I should have been sent off but he didn't know what to do; he just shit it!

"Refs turned against me many times. They didn't like me and enjoyed winding me up. Uriah Rennie was one top ref I had many run ins with and, for me, he made a lot of big errors. Sometimes refs laughed in my face winding me up even more; in certain games if I was in the ref's ear, I felt they would give decisions to the opposition to get their own back. I honestly think some referees and linesmen were scared of me. On the positive side, Jeff Winter was one official I did get on with and respected. You could talk to him and he would swear back at us, but you didn't mess with him.

"I do know what a difficult job it is though. Martin O'Neill made me referee a five-a-side game in training – it was one of the hardest things I've ever done!"

We put on brave faces at our post-match reception at the Sketchley Grange Hotel, near Hinckley, where all the lads promised we'd be promoted as champions in 12 months. There was no way we'd leave our fate to the play offs again, we said. That evening was also memorable for what happened when we let our hair down and had a few drinks. I was one of the last lads up with my brother-in-law Neil drowning my sorrows. It was early morning and we were sitting with Janet Elsom, wife of City chairman John, who was consoling me as we sat on a settee in reception. After all, it had been a massive achievement for us to get to Wembley for two successive play off finals. She had her arm round me, then suddenly embraced me with a kiss. Neil reacted quickly to end the moment and took me for a walk. In all honestly, it was all innocent stuff.

My contract was up for renewal that summer and I could have hitched a ride into the Premier League easily enough with several clubs wanting to sign me. That was a time when converted centre backs were making plenty of headlines with Paul Warhurst doing the business at Sheffield Wednesday and Chris Sutton moving from Norwich to big-spending Blackburn Rovers after also making the switch from back to front. But my future at Leicester City was never in doubt. Our Wembley torture made me even more determined to follow my dream and help the Foxes back where we belong. A four-year deal was put on the table and it didn't take long for me to agree terms as there was still unfinished business for Walshy at Leicester City. Little did I know who I'd be playing up front with come the new season in August!

Mention David Speedie to City fans and you ran for cover – that was before he signed for us on a free transfer from Southampton. It was a brave move by Brian Little but one I backed. He knew that, of all the City lads, I had most reason to dislike the bloke after the way he'd done me at Wembley and other run ins I had with him over the years. But I recognised one thing: it was always better to have a guy like Speedo on your side rather than the opposition. He was a quick-thinking terrier of a striker who knew exactly where the back of the net was. Defenders didn't like to play against him.

I had a score to settle and quickly made my point. I walked into the dressing room shortly after Speedo arrived and he was on the treatment table. He passed a sarcastic remark in my direction and I erupted. I grabbed him by the throat and pinned him down on the table. It did the trick. Apart from a few well publicised social evenings, we didn't have too much trouble with Speedo afterwards even though he was a nightmare with a drink inside him. We even built a reasonable partnership where it really mattered – on the pitch.

The hell's strikers of a combo of Speedie and Walsh was responsible for eight of our first 12 goals as we made a good start to the new campaign. I also enjoyed scoring a cracker past former City goalkeeper Martin Hodge in a 6-1 thrashing of Rochdale in the Coca Cola Cup.

Then disaster struck. The injury I suffered during a 2-0 defeat against Middlesbrough at Ayresome Park could have ended my career but for the brilliance of surgeon Angus Strover over in Droitwich. As soon as I was carried off on a stretcher, I knew it was bad – and Brian Little feared the worst. It took 10 days to confirm our fears as, there was so much bleeding inside my knee, scans couldn't detect the damage. Mr Strover confirmed the terrible news when I went to a clinic after it had settled – I'd completely ruptured my anterior cruciate ligament (ACL). An MRI scan showed it was completely torn from the bone but Mr Strover lifted my spirits straightaway. He said he'd have me playing football again in seven or eight months. Such confidence gave me great hope at a very, very difficult time. Cruciate ligament damage is the injury players fear most. You have to marvel at the technology that got the likes of Alan Shearer, Paul Gascoigne and, yes, Steve Walsh playing again.

Mr Strover did the operation - a complicated job involving using part of my patella tendon as the new ligament – and I hoped for the best. The official forecast was that I would be out of action until the end of the season - but it can take 12 months to get your full strength back. I saw pictures of the fantastic job the surgeon did. The knee was as clean as a whistle. Now I needed to do my bit. I did vow though that I'd quit if I could never again be the same player. I didn't fancy being a passenger at Leicester City.

Watching from the stands wasn't ideal but, at least, the lads were going well. We had the fireworks to go top of the table with a 3-0 victory over Southend on Bonfire Night. A couple of disappointing defeats followed and it was really frustrating to be on the sidelines as we tackled Bully and co when Wolves came to Filbert Street. The striker ran riot in the first half - even though I wasn't playing, I felt the urge to kick him! But we got some of our own back as the lad who'd been signed to cover for me, Iwan Roberts, became an instant City hero with two goals on his debut. A 2-2 draw brought one priceless point and one unforgettable toothless grin!

I was back in light training as early as the New Year but getting onto the field seemed light years away. The rehab from an ACL injury is one of the longest and frustrating of all. One thing in my favour was that the knee wasn't put into plaster after the operation, so I got the chance to bend it almost from day one. Believe me, the first fortnight or so was very painful but, at least, there was some mobility in it and I began to hit every landmark in my recovery ahead of schedule. I was cycling, light jogging in straight lines, then kicking a ball - all ahead of schedule. I was on my way back. But playing again as soon as I did after such a serious injury did me no long term favours. It was crazy to be honest as my thigh muscles weren't back to normal. I should have waited far longer. The knee and the leg weren't nearly strong enough – and I knew it. I just put my hand up and said I was ready because I was desperate to be involved in the end of season drama.

The season became our usual emotional rollercoaster. We were back on top in early February but given a 4-0 mauling by Forest at the City Ground. It wasn't much better when we visited the other side of the Trent as Notts County whipped us 4-1 at Meadow Lane. Little was keen to reintroduce me to football his way and decided a few minutes of first team action would be far more useful than several games in the reserves. My long awaited comeback came in a midweek match against Pompey at Filbo when the floodlights failed and we were 3-0 down by half time. At least I drew some cheers from the City faithful when I came on in the 63rd minute but it wasn't the most promising of nights for me either. First thing I did was make a late challenge on Portsmouth's goalkeeper. I thought it was ok but it got me a yellow card. Then I was involved again in a 1-1 draw at Watford. Thanks to Mr Strover and my own naivety, I was back – and, unbelievably, Wembley was beckoning yet again.

A six-game unbeaten run meant we finished the league campaign with 73 points. Alongside us in the dreaded play offs were Millwall, Tranmere and Derby County.

Surely not? The thought of an end of season shootout between the two great East Midlands rivals was too good – or bad – to even think about. I promised Little three weeks before the play off final that, should we make it to Wembley, I'd be fit and ready. Well, ready anyway! Even by my pain-defying standards, I'd have probably settled for building up my knee and preparing for the following season but for that last crack at getting into the Premier League. I knew I was no more than 60 or 70 per cent fit but adrenalin would take me through on the big day.

There was one big obstacle to overcome before we could think of Wembley and that was a durable Tranmere Rovers side in a two legged semi final. I couldn't even save myself for Wembley; I just had to play and try to help us to get there. Brian left me out completely from the first leg and gambled we could get a result - it worked, a scrappy 0-0 draw at Prenton Park meaning we were slight favourites going back to Filbert Street. I was ready to put my body on the line for as long as humanly possible in the return and got a piece of the action this time. 'Sticks' Ormondroyd made himself even more popular as a play off specialist by giving us the lead. Tranmere equalised and the tie was up for grabs before in the dying minutes Speedo bundled the ball over the line to take the limelight with me right behind him ready to grab it myself had he missed. That was the final curtain for one of City's most unlikely double acts. For the ever-unpredictable Speedie then got himself sent off, ruling him out of the final, and never played for City again. The fiery striker's spell with us was short and not exactly sweet, but at least he left Filbert Street a lot more popular than when he arrived.

Derby saw off Millwall very convincingly in the other semi, following up a 2-0 home victory with a 3-1 success at The Den. Roy McFarland's side wasn't short of individual talent with Tommy Johnson, Marco Gabbiadini, Craig Short and our old colleague Paul Kitson among their ranks. Worse still, we had no fewer than eight players injured. Make that nine including me – but the manager took a calculated gamble and gave me the shirt. I'll make another confession: Derby were by far the better footballing side. Even the most Blue blinkered fan at Wembley would have to admit that. But nobody could deny we deserved to get to the Premier League. For our squad, it was third time lucky at Wembley; as for me, I was getting lucky for a long time afterwards!

The Rams could have been a goal or two up even before Gabbiadini struck after 27 minutes. Jimmy Willis cleared one off the line and the same Derby striker missed after being sent clear of our defence. We needed a break and got one with four minutes of the first half left. Mike Whitlow lifted our spirits with a thunderbolt that brought a brilliant save from Martin Taylor but the Derby goalkeeper didn't do so well when Gary Coatsworth lofted a ball into his area. He was grounded as I rose above him and Iwan Roberts to plant the ball towards goal but Derby defender Paul Williams, a few yards from the line, should really have cleared it. Somehow he misjudged the spin on the ball completely and we were level at 1-1. As I reeled away I had to look twice to believe it was a goal – now, come on!

Second half brought the usual few incidents that could have turned the game either way. We feared the worst when Simon Grayson brought down the speedy Johnson just outside our penalty area. Referee Roger Milford could have produced a red card as Grayson was the last man but contented himself with yellow. American international John Harkes missed a sitter when he pulled the ball wide of goal with only goalkeeper Gavin Ward to beat. Then came THAT moment; the one that changed my life. It came from probably our best move all afternoon. I knocked it down to Joachim who swept the ball out wide left to the overlapping Grayson whose quality whipped in cross was met by Sticks launching himself into a tremendous header at the near post. For a split second I thought he'd scored. Yet instinct and momentum led me to follow the ball in. Taylor's save was fantastic but there I was beating two defenders to the loose ball and steering it into the empty net with my right peg. Next came mayhem; my head exploded. I relive that feeling every time I see the photo – the one everyone associates me with. Scoring any goal is exhilarating but getting the last gasp winner against Derby at Wembley to put us into the Premier League for the very first time was unbelievable. I can still see myself reeling away to the corner flag and our fans going mental - the euphoria, elation and adrenalin rush was sensational. I never stopped scoring for ages after that. I was popular enough with the ladies before Wembley but AD (After Derby) was something else. Put it this way, I was far too much in demand for the comfort of my marriage as ladies couldn't keep their hands off the guy who silenced The Rams!

Those two goals probably assured my place in City's Hall of Fame but inside I was hurting a little as Simon Grayson lifted the trophy. No offence to 'Larry', who is a great mate, but that should have been me. I felt Brian should have reinstated me for the game. I deserved my captaincy back and, to this day, still feel slightly offended. But I wasn't going to argue with the manager as he had his reasons. I gave my boots away to Jon Agar, a nice lad I keep in touch with. I make him an offer every year but he won't sell them. He gave me them back once to take to Wembley for the Palace play-off final which was a nice touch. I should have told him I'd lost them! The celebrations were great all the way back to Leicester, up the M1 and long into the night at Sketchley Grange. I was a hero everyone wanted a piece of including the press. I even did an interview at 8am with Sabras Radio.

ASK any City fan of a certain age for the name of the club's biggest icon and Walshy will surely top the list. That says everything about his popularity more than 13 years after the end of his playing days at Filbert Street.

But it wasn't just the Blue Army who idolised him; he was the football commentator's dream too. Instantly recognisable and with an uncanny knack of being at the very heart of whatever was happening on the pitch, he was also invariably willing to give an interview.

Walshy provided me with some of my most memorable moments behind the Radio Leicester microphone – the controversial clash with David Speedie against Blackburn at Wembley and that agonising night at Boro when he collapsed with an injury that would have finished many a player are high among them.

But, if ever there was a poll for the station's favourite sporting moment, it would have to be his winning goal against Derby County, also at Wembley. His close mate Gary Mills, who was unable to play through injury, almost took the roof off our commentary box because he knew just how much the big guy had gone through to even be playing that afternoon.

The joy of the many thousands of City fans was increased still further by the fact it was Walshy, their hero, who did it. That's why it is great to see him back working at Leicester City today, where he truly belongs.

NEVILLE FOULGER,
Leicester City's Radio Leicester commentator 1990-2004.

Had I been sensible and listened to my body, there's no way I'd have set foot on the Wembley turf, let alone become Leicester City's hero. It came back to me all over again this May when I celebrated 20 years since that amazing afternoon. Twenty years? It only seems like 20 minutes in a way, but then so much has happened…... Just a few days later Derby got done again by a last minute goal in their play off final against Harry Redknapp's QPR. For the first time in my career I actually wanted Derby to win as you can't beat the rivalry of local derby games.

I paid the price for coming back too quick. But, first, I scarcely had a day off in the summer as I trained daily even on my family holiday in Marbella - between a few heavy sessions, of course - to ensure the knee was stronger for the Premier League kick off. I even chose the apartment because it was handy for the local gym which didn't impress Debbie too much.

Little raised expectations when talented Notts County midfielder Mark Draper took our transfer record up to £1.25m although I was more interested in the signing of central defender Nicky Mohan from Boro. That gave me the hint I was going to play up front in the top flight; a move confirmed when Brian Little told Blue Army News he was linking me up once again with Jocky.

Sceptics said City were always among the favourites to be relegated straight back down from the Premier League. A side scraping through the play offs is always even more fancied for the chop than those that have been automatically promoted. But that's not how we felt. Like England fans preparing for a World Cup, the closer we got to kick off, the more we rated our chances of upsetting a few teams. We had a very good young manager, an unbeatable team spirit and our fair share of talent, Draper included. I lived for getting back into the top league with Leicester City; now that had become reality and I was 'Top Man' with the fans, I was determined to make the absolute most of it. Yet that dream crashed both for City and for me within the space of a few weeks.

We ran out to rapturous applause, from a full house of more than 20,000 fans, for our opening match in front of the Sky TV cameras on a sunny Sunday afternoon against Newcastle United but the story of my season had been written before we kicked off again at Blackburn Rovers in midweek.

We lost 3-1 against the Geordies, a match I honestly think we could have won. But there were tell tale signs of something more significant. My knee had been rock solid as we prepared for the season and I was fit and raring to go. Yet I felt the joint open up in the Newcastle game and still didn't read the warning signs. I felt a cracking and popping inside my joint in the warm up before the Blackburn game and should never have started. My bravery, if that's what you call it, was a big, big mistake. By the time I came off injured, I couldn't run a yard and had torn my cartilage in four places. And, yes, 100 per cent I could trace the problem back to my original injury and say I'd done too much too soon. After the game in which I still managed to hit the post a kind Kenny Dalglish came to see me and wished me well - what a legend!

So instead of looking forward to the third game – a very tasty clash with our great rivals and fellow promoted Forest at the City Ground – I was coming round from yet another op. But this was more than just another injury blow. I'd rebuilt my confidence during the long road to recovery; now I was back to square one. That was a very hard psychological hit to take. Shortly after that Jocky broke a bone in his foot and he, too, was sidelined for a long period as our season started to fold.

By the time I returned for another televised match against Manchester City, the club had suffered another mortal blow, the loss of Brian Little. For a lot of fellow Foxes fans Little's move to Aston Villa still seems like yesterday. There was anger and disappointment at Filbert Street about the way the manager departed. Speculation mounted daily that Villa chairman Doug Ellis wanted Little to replace Big Ron Atkinson who'd been sacked after a poor run of results. City chairman Martin George stood his ground and said Little was staying – the manager himself didn't give anything away. Next thing we knew Little had resigned and taken up the post at Villa Park.

It hurt me that Little even considered leaving Filbert Street after what he achieved. But, after talking the issue through with him at his house, I can honestly say I don't blame him. Brian was and is a Villa man and told me "Walshy, I would never have thought about it had it been any other team than Villa." My good friend and manager was gone but I could handle his reasons. I put myself in his shoes. Had I ever been offered the Leicester City job, I'd have moved like a shot – wouldn't have mattered where I was or what I was doing. That's because I'm a 'True Blue'. Managers can go through the motions when they say it was such a hard decision. But, for Brian Little, it was both the hardest and simplest move he ever made. The guy has a very genuine and deep affection for Leicester City and was completely torn apart when fans accused him of being a 'Judas' and 'liar' when he brought Villa to Filbert Street for a league game a few weeks later. He only went with his heart – as I would have done. I trust, given time to reflect on what happened, most City fans still have fond memories of Brian's time with us. I certainly do. Up to Martin O'Neill's appointment, the best three years of my Leicester City career were spent with Brian Little as manager.

O'Neill's name was first linked with the Leicester job, along with Mike Walker and, ironically, Big Ron, as we were looking for Little's successor. But he stayed loyal to Wycombe Wanderers, the team he'd brought up from Non League and built his reputation as a manager with. Instead the job went to Mark McGhee, another name that raises strong emotions among Leicester City fans.

I'm not going to slag McGhee off despite what happened. I always got on well with him, although I was closer to his coach Colin Lee. But there was a big, big difference between Little's departure to Villa and McGhee jumping ship in favour of Wolves, as happened the following season. Fans saw them both as Judases and I can understand their point of view. But, whereas Little was tempted by his first football love, McGhee was merely ambitious and out for himself. He never had the same affinity with Leicester City as Little -and the feeling was mutual. I don't blame McGhee for our relegation that sad season – we finished second bottom with a miserable 29 points and rarely looked capable of staying in the Premier League. To be honest, we needed everything to go in our favour to make a good fist of it. Making a bad start and losing the manager set us off in the wrong direction and we never really recovered. McGhee did his best bringing in £1m striker Mark Robins, from Norwich City, in a bid to find a top finisher during a time when I was missing – but it wasn't enough.

At first, I didn't get on too well with McGhee. There was the issue of my injury worries and I didn't know whether he wanted me in his team; perhaps he thought I was bigger at Leicester City than him? There was an arrogance about McGhee in the way he related with the lads. He always had to be number one and didn't mind showing off to prove it. I remember being in Germany for a pre season tour when all McGhee wanted was to get to the Hugo Boss factory and Adidas to buy himself loads of Hugo Boss suits and trainers. He was a bit selfish like that. That wasn't going to be a problem though as long as he got results. We had a good tour in Germany in which we did a lot of fitness work and came back fit and strong. Better still, we also got out for a couple of big nights. Unusually for us, there was no trouble.

My status as a senior player got me into a muddle with McGhee which almost resulted in me walking out the door. I always backed the manager in what he was trying to do – including the discipline – but I was also one of the lads. There were reports one or two players had gone out drinking on tour whereas I knew they'd gone no further than McDonalds which serves nothing stronger than a milkshake. I stood up for my team mates because I knew they hadn't done anything wrong and McGhee wasn't happy with my attitude. To say I was disappointed when he called me in for a chat and questioned where I stood was the understatement of the year. I'd always been free to speak my mind and couldn't see why that should change. Surely McGhee wasn't questioning my commitment to City? I was desperate to get out there on the pitch and help us launch another promotion bid. Anyway, the issue blew over and I got on much better with McGhee in the weeks that followed.

McGhee's style was to play football. He certainly helped our midfielders gain confidence on the ball. Playing it out from the back was ok from a personal point of view, as I was quite comfortable on the ball, but I'd still question it. Why pass the ball a few yards forward when the next player would be closed down instantly and subjected to a crunching tackle? To be honest, it didn't really work at the level we were playing at. After being effective rather than pretty under Brian Little, we were in real danger of being just the opposite in McGhee's charge. Our opening home game against Stoke City was a great example. We lit up Filbert Street with our passing style but still ended up on the wrong end of a 3-2 scoreline. I did have the consolation of scoring City's second goal when I spotted former team mate Carl Muggleton lining up his defensive wall and caught him cold with a quick free kick.

McGhee's signings reflected his outlook. Steve Corica, signed from a Sydney-based club was a talented addition and Scott Taylor, bought from McGhee's former club Reading for £500,000, was another ball playing midfielder with plenty of energy. Add in Garry Parker as skipper and there was never going to be any shortage of ball playing class.

The manager's strangest signing had to be Zelijko Kalac, who will always be remembered as 'Spider' by City fans. The Australian goalkeeper, a 6'7" giant, was clearly a gamble on McGhee's part. My first impression was that he had an attitude problem. We'd line up to shoot against both Kalac and Kevin Poole in shooting practise - they'd fly past the Aussie, whilst we could never score against Pooley. Kalac would then grab the ball and smash it away in frustration. More worrying still, it soon became clear the giant couldn't catch as he virtually threw in all three goals in a League Cup defeat at home to Bolton.

The McGhee signing I was closest to was Mike Galloway, who joined us on loan from Celtic. He was a tough midfielder, who never pulled out of tackles. Off the field, he was quite unpredictable, too, although I always got on with him as he liked his drink. One night in the pub he managed to get an eye injury from a pool cue but that was nothing compared with the accident that ended his career. He was involved in a terrible car crash, hitting a vehicle full of breeze blocks head on. There were suspicions he had been drinking but that was for the authorities to determine. Anyway he was in the Leicester Royal Infirmary for weeks in a coma fighting for his life with Celtic manager Tommy Burns coming over to see him. He was in a bad state having severed arteries in his back and spine and broken his thighbone. He had to have rods inserted through his pelvis. I visited him every day knowing he was never going to kick a ball again. It was awful to see. Once I visited him in the Royal after training and could hear Mike screaming. The nurse said I couldn't see him as he'd been like this for 12 hours; rods in his pelvis had caused an infection and no drugs would help him. I pinned up an image of me scoring the winning goal against Derby which he liked. He later told me I was close to him when I had gone. As I left in my car it was pouring down but a song came on the radio that always reminds me of Mick – *The Ghost of Sex and You* by Mike and the Mechanics. It cut me up in the car; you play it and see how you feel. Walshy didn't get too emotional in those days but this did me. I played it time and time again.

Mike was a loner by nature who got himself into a few scrapes. Our friendship survived even though he borrowed some money off me and wasn't able to pay it back. After the crash, Celtic gave him a testimonial. He then came to Leicester to see me. We went out for a few drinks and shared a room at the Holiday Inn together. The scars on his legs were very visible from the top of his thighs to his ankles. "I don't remember seeing any of them," I said to him as he was hiding himself from me, I knew he had a severed nerve in his spine that gave him a dropped foot but not these scars. He replied "Walshy, I tried to kill myself one night after a drink! I was in the kitchen trying to keep a ball up but couldn't do it so got a carving knife out the drawer and tried to end it by chopping my legs off." It was like a scene from SAW apparently. He must have been so depressed and was found slumped on the floor by his girlfriend. That's not something I could ever do but he was obviously tortured in his mind and I felt for him. I've lost touch with Mike, who has had a couple of managerial appointments since, but I wish him all the best.

After crossing swords with Bully again when Wolves came to Filbert Street and left empty handed thanks to a Mike Whitlow goal, my new partnership with Jimmy

Willis was interrupted as I suffered another setback with my knee – the left one this time. McGhee had Mick Hickman, an old school Sergeant Major-type coach, rip into me one day and put me through hell knowing my knee was damaged. In the end it locked up completely and I ended up back with Mr Strover in Droitwich for another op. This time it was the underneath of my kneecap flaking away. There wasn't too much damage but it still meant a month out of action.

We topped the table early that season, mostly because of our excellent form away from home. Yet a 3-1 defeat at Huddersfield Town highlighted a weakness in McGhee's total football. We had Scott Taylor and Steve Corica pushing up and relied a great deal on Parker being the source of supply from midfield. It was great when we had space to feed Parker but not when the opposition started flooding through onto our defence as we lacked the real pace in there. The balance between footballing ability and steel wasn't right, in my view.

That all became irrelevant however when McGhee suddenly – and disgracefully – walked out on us. Again, we went through the farce of the usual denials from both City chairman Martin George and McGhee himself as rumours he was on his way to replace Graham Taylor at Wolves began to circulate. Our anger was fuelled by disbelief. Surely this could not happen to us again so soon after Brian Little's departure? But there were clear differences in the way McGhee treated us. Unlike Brian, he didn't bother to explain his situation to us. He just upped and left with us still very well placed in the table and knowing full well how badly City fans would take it. I felt sorry for Brian Little for the stick he took and I hope I did my bit both back then and now to speak up for him; but I have no sympathy for McGhee. Yet he was no great loss, was he? Things never worked out for him at Wolves and he turned into a journeyman manager drifting from club to club never really doing the business. McGhee leaving just opened the door for the most successful manager in our proud history. Enter King Martin O'Neill – but first there was a panto to sort out. I'm not talking about the Christmas cards the club sent out still bearing the image of McGhee with the sickeningly inaccurate message of 'the future's Marked out' but the dramas that occurred before O'Neill took his place in the hot seat.

Among the first candidates was one Steve Walsh. I was part of the caretaker team alongside David Nish and Chris Turner who took charge of City at Southend. I honestly thought back then – as I did later – I could do a job for Leicester City. The players respected and would have played for me. But I was wrong. Working my way back from yet another injury, I could be forgiven for thinking I didn't have too many more playing days on my clock. Yet had I gone into management, I'd have missed out on the very best years of my career.

Instead it was a tale of two managers with Norwich City connections – ironic as the Canaries were our visitors for our next match in front of the Central TV cameras at Filbert Street. First choice appeared to be Mike Walker, a legend at Carrow Road before finding the going far tougher when he got his big job at Everton. He travelled to Leicester for an interview and looked odds on to be confirmed as our new boss. Yet strange things were happening back in Norwich. O'Neill had only been there five minutes after leaving Wycombe Wanderers yet fallen out badly with chairman Robert Chase. We were told he had refused to travel with the team to Leicester and made it clear he should have accepted the City post when it was offered to him a few months earlier. All that was forgotten during a thrilling rollercoaster afternoon in which I made my return at the back and witnessed a great performance by a City legend of the future, Emile Heskey. We were 2-0 down in the first half but young Heskey inspired our comeback and scored a brilliant winning goal to send our fans home happy – but slightly confused!

Everything was made clear within the next 48 hours. Walker had indeed been pipped for the post by Martin O'Neill who began his reign at Leicester City on December 21, 1995. So I welcomed yet another manager to Filbert Street, our fifth permanent boss since 1990. But this was going to be different. Or was it?

Chapter Six

Something Inside So Strong

Lifting a major trophy in front of the Leicester faithful is better than larruping any woman!

IT'S PROBABLY fair to say that Steve Walsh was Leicester City in the 1990s. As much as Brian Little, who took the club to three Championship play-off Finals, or Martin O'Neill, who guided the club to three League Cup Finals, Walshy, there for all but one of these Wembley events, summed up the club.

He was an Errol Flynn type of hero, swashbuckling and daring. He was a fearsomely competitive centre-back, and a makeshift centre-forward, whom the opposition, whether Arsenal or Tranmere, would rather wasn't on the team sheet.

Coming up for corners, he attacked the ball with skill, heart and a rare determination. The number of goals he either scored or laid on for others is apt testimony to his considerable abilities. As a captain he led by example, brave and uncompromising, never giving up on a Leicester cause, however hopeless it might seem.

As a Leicester fan from birth, Walshy was always a favourite of mine. Sadly we never played on the same side. Happily, I can't recall a competitive fixture against him.

But I have great respect for the big man. He's in my all time Leicester best team — a true City legend.

GARY LINEKER OBE, Leicester City and England legend

Something Inside So Strong – I love that song! Nothing better sums up my feelings about our great era under Martin O'Neill. Labi Siffre's voice and words came with me on the team bus, wherever we travelled, so all the lads got a reminder of the fantastic spirit we had as a team. Ok, it wasn't written about a football team but the message was the same – I dug deeper than ever before for O'Neill's City when my body was constantly telling me enough was enough.

O'Neill was the best manager I ever played for and almost certainly the finest in the proud history of Leicester City Football Club – but, I'll tell you this, even King Martin was no magician. One image from March 30 1996 will probably be remembered by every City fan of a certain age. It should, to be honest, be put on a postcard and sent to every chairman thinking of hastily sacking their manager. There was O'Neill, our new and very frustrated manager, under verbal attack from angry Foxes fans after a shocking 2-0 home defeat against modest Sheffield United. No mistake about it, that was a bad, bad day. I held my hands up - I was awful. The team as a whole was as bad as I could ever remember. But the demo against O'Neill and the board wasn't just about defeat by Howard Kendall's Blades. That was the straw that broke the camel's back. We'd won just three out of 18 matches in league and cup since O'Neill took charge. From being well positioned in third place, just two points behind leaders Sunderland, we were now a huge 20 points adrift in ninth. Even reaching the play offs looked to be beyond us. What was going wrong?

I can't tell you all the answers. But what I do know is that Martin's first three months at Leicester City showed just how easily a manager can be judged before getting his feet under the table. The guy was well up for the challenge at Leicester. He spoke at his opening press conference about being 'ecstatic' about being here and the fact he'd walked out on Norwich to join us lifted our spirits after what we suffered. But the chemistry of the team he took over wasn't quite right. We all know the O'Neill way; never the ultra direct style the critics spoke of but a lot different to McGhee's free flowing methods, that's for sure. Our new boss wanted to build his side on solid physical foundations, rather like his mentor Brian Clough. Strong centre half, strong central midfield player and a big centre forward were his building blocks and spine of the team. The side he took over from Mark McGhee wasn't like that. We played out from the back, fed Garry Parker in midfield and flooded forward as a team. This latest culture change took time - and the addition of O'Neill's kind of players – before it really took shape. Incredible to think but time very nearly ran out on him that very afternoon.

Could Martin O'Neill have walked out of Leicester City and his place in our hearts? Yes, that really could have happened. He's a very principled man, who doesn't quit easily, despite his problems at Norwich. But he hated being abused in that way. Yet the very fact he faced supporters, probably hugely embarrassed now they ever called for his head, tells me another thing. He hated the idea of failing even more. He used that 'rock bottom' experience as the lowest he and we could go and turned it into a positive. There was 'Something Inside So Strong' in Martin O'Neill as well as Steve Walsh - one reason we were such a great team.

I knew that, as long as I could drag my aching body onto that pitch, I was in O'Neill's plans. I was the strong man he was looking for in his defence, all the more so after he brought in Julian Watts from David Pleat's Sheffield Wednesday just before transfer deadline. I formed as good a partnership with Wattsy as with anyone since Russell Osman ten years earlier. Like Watts, the manager's other signings grew on the players and the fans almost daily without being greeted with huge headlines and expectations. Neil Lennon, a £750,000 signing from Crewe, was the man of steel O'Neill needed in the middle of the park and he was joined by my good pal Muzzy Izzet, very highly rated at Chelsea but still a relative unknown as he was playing his football in the reserves. We all knew almost instantly that O'Neill had unearthed a rare diamond in Muzzy. Striker Steve Claridge was another greeted with mixed feelings – at least by the fans. He looked every inch the football journeyman when we plucked him away from Birmingham City for £1.25m. But he was just the right player to give young Emile Heskey the support he needed up front.

We had already enjoyed one or two good afternoons under O'Neill – well, one in particular. We'd gone nine games without victory when we rolled up at Molineux for a reunion with you-know-who – and I'm not talking about Bully. Nobody at Leicester City, let alone me, needed motivating to put one over on McGhee. Heskey helped himself to a couple of good goals and Iwan Roberts got the other as we won 3-2. Each time we scored, I aimed my celebration at the manager who walked out on us. He made silly gestures back as if to say 'why me?' No way was I going to miss my chance to rub those golden moments right down his throat.

Our first home win under O'Neill wasn't quite so memorable. Heskey got another couple as we saw off Grimsby Town 2-1 but the success was marred by a major row between skipper Parker and manager O'Neill. Parker was the one who threw the tea cups but there could only be one winner. O'Neill dropped him from the side, put him on the transfer list and handed the armband back to me. It says a lot, however, for both parties that, although the relationship between player and manager seemed dead and buried, Parker returned to play a full part in our success story that followed.

There was much talk about the poor quality of the Filbert Street pitch that season – a frequent McGhee excuse when trying to play perfect football. Since the Carling Stand had been built and blocked off much of the sunlight, it wasn't good. But when Ipswich completed a quick double over us with a 2-0 victory in our backyard, it was no time to make excuses. What we desperately needed was a victory. Just over 12,000 watched us do just that against Millwall a week before the Blades arrived in town for that fateful day.

Looking back, the Sheffield United fiasco did us all a favour. It meant hitting rock bottom, but still being ninth in the table. I know O'Neill treated it as a day not to be forgotten but to learn from. It tells you a lot about his character that he made a phone call to one of the fans who abused him on the very evening when we turned such a disappointing situation into end-of-season triumph.

Successive away trips to London to face strong Charlton and Crystal Palace – sides we had to beat but were ahead of us in the table - looked like the last thing we needed. But somehow we fancied the green, green grass of The Valley almost the moment we arrived - a nice change from the mud of home. Claridge curled a great goal into the corner of the Charlton net in the first half and Wattsy and I did the business when they came back at us after the break. I remember Martin telling me how fantastic I was after sliding in desperation to kick a goal bound effort off the line. It was much the same story at Palace where Roberts gave us the lead and again we resisted a strong onslaught to claim all three points.

Walshy on my best ever game: "People will presume it was that Wembley final against Derby County, but my performance against Crystal Palace in the league game shortly before we beat them at the national stadium was better in my book. Palace have always been a physical and direct side in my memory and they threw everything at us at Selhurst Park. Even their goalkeeper was strolling up to the halfway line to loft the ball into our box. Crosses were raining in on us from all angles and this was a match we simply had to win. But I never missed a header all afternoon – not one. I felt totally in the zone and on top of my game as we held out to win a vital match 1-0. I must have headed 200 balls and my timing was never better.

"The only blot on my day was breaking my right thumb joint in four places when hit by a fiercely hit cross shortly after half time. I played on for the final 40 minutes and surgery was delayed because O'Neill wanted me in contention for the play offs. I had to play 10 games, including the final ironically against Palace, with my thumb dislocating every time I went to ground. But this was never going to stop me lifting a trophy. I had a scrap towards the end with David Hopkin, the Palace midfielder who reckoned he was a hard guy. I got him back at Wembley with a crunching tackle when I took the ball and made sure I got a good piece of him as well. I think everyone in the crowd heard the noise it made. Walshy payback time!"

Two wins and six points was a great morale boost but setbacks the following week showed we still weren't going to have things all our own way. Roberts was stretchered off with cracked ribs as West Bromwich Albion stunned us by scoring an injury time winner at Filbert Street.

I was suspended for going over the 20 points mark but was pleased to see Claridge bag a couple of goals as we beat Oldham 2-0 at Filbert Street. Despite our wobbles, we were still in seventh spot and only outside the play off zone on goal difference. With just three games left, we needed our home form to be spot on – and it was. I returned to score the opening goal as we beat Huddersfield 2-1 and Birmingham City went home with their tails between their legs after being beaten 3-0.

Ipswich weren't giving up without a fight and their midweek victory meant we went into our final match against relegation-threatened Watford still praying the Tractor Men slipped up against Millwall or Charlton failed to win their final game. They were ahead on goal difference and barring a goal glut would qualify for the play offs ahead of us with a home victory. There's nothing you can do other than do the business yourselves and that's how we approached it. We needed to beat Watford to put us in pole position and it was a tight, tight game against Graham Taylor's men. That was when Muzzy Izzet turned himself into an instant City hero by heading the winner and, with both other results going our way, we ended up finishing fifth. Never in doubt, eh? Graham Taylor shook my hand and wished us all the best – great sport, Graham.

We were so lucky to have a top class goalkeeper in that Leicester City side in Kevin Poole. I saw at first hand the incredible dedication that served him so well in his remarkable career. Pooley is one of the very few players to be registered with a football club at the age of 50 as goalkeeping coach at Burton Albion. That didn't happen by accident. When the rest of us had a day off, Pooley was in every morning. He even had two days a week with Peter Bonetti and, as with all the best goalkeepers, hated picking the ball out of the back of his net in training. Very rarely did anyone get one past Pooley! He came into his own with one of the best saves I ever saw in my career during our play off semi final against Stoke City at Filbert Street. That came during the first few minutes of a tie that finished without a goal, leaving most pundits reckoning Stoke were favourites for Wembley. Even I thought we were up against it that time.

The second leg, however, was a triumph for O'Neill after he patched up his differences with Garry Parker. The midfielder was still popular with City fans despite becoming a regular on the bench after his bust up with the boss. But O'Neill chose the Victoria Ground to restore Parker to the starting line up for the crucial return. We were the better side second time around and it was Parker's classy finish that took us to Wembley yet again and a quick rematch with Crystal Palace.

Could a season that saw us kicked in the stomach by McGhee's departure and stutter and stagger before coming to life again under O'Neill yet finish with a dream ticket to the Premier League? One thing was in our favour – make that five! We had Kevin Poole, Simon Grayson, Mike Whitlow and Colin Hill and I who had all been to Wembley before and tasted the unique atmosphere and tension of the occasion. Incredibly, the Blue Army numbered 38,500 - about 5,000 more than the opposition – and it was our fourth play off final in five years. The national stadium had become our second home.

Our 1-0 victory at Selhurst Park a few weeks earlier was another factor in our favour. We took everything they could throw at us on their own patch and never gave an inch. Many folk fancied Palace but we were confident. I only played after more painkilling injections for a back problem that had troubled me during the last few weeks of the season. But no way was I going to miss out on such a huge match. That became my favourite Wembley final in the sense it was our best team performance. We couldn't argue we were the better side against Blackburn, Swindon or Derby but there was no doubt we deserved our place in the Premier League that Spring Bank Holiday Monday. The way it was achieved, however, still has hairs standing up on the back of my neck when I think about it.

Palace went ahead when Andy Roberts shot home after 20 minutes before we launched wave after wave of attack on their goal. We had the initiative for long periods and it seemed only a matter of time before we equalised. Yet Pooley still had to make two brilliant saves on the break to keep us in contention and, with the clock ticking by, the unthinkable was very possible. Then came the first edition of the Steve Walsh and Muzzy Izzet show. I supplied a long through pass and Muzzy broke into the Palace box where he was brought down by Mark Edworthy. Definite peno! Who stepped up to take the crucial spot kick but Garry Parker, the player we thought was finished at Leicester just a few weeks before. Agonisingly, Nigel Martyn got a touch to his kick but it still had enough power to find the corner of the net and we were level with 15 minutes of normal time left. Only one team was going to win it from then on – but could we make our dominance count before the unbearable tension of a penalty shootout?

Had it gone to spot kicks, I wouldn't have taken one. I went off totally exhausted a few minutes before the end of extra time but it was another substitution in the final seconds for which O'Neill will be remembered. If there was one area of the game in which Spider Kalac could hold a candle to our Pooley it was from 12 yards, although I would still have backed Pooley to save more. I'm sure O'Neill, the master of mind games, used the chance to confuse Palace by bringing on a substitute goalkeeper just when they were thinking how to beat Poole. As it turned out, Spider never touched the ball – probably no bad thing! Instead we scored a remarkable winner with just a couple of seconds left on the clock. I still wonder how Claridge did it. What a strike! Many people think he shinned it, not me. It found its way past Martyn into the top corner like slow motion. When the final whistle went a few seconds later, Martin and I turned to each other and embraced. It was a very emotional moment during which the manager told me, heart to heart, just how well I'd done that season and I thanked him for pulling off virtually a football miracle.

When I summoned the energy to go up those steps and collect the trophy it was my proudest moment so far apart from the Derby winner. I remember each and every step with scarves being rapped around me and being kissed by the fans. The medal was put around my neck, I kissed the cup twice and the whole place erupted. The feeling was just indescribable.

I was quoted afterwards as saying that could easily have been my last ever game for Leicester City – and I stand by that. I was in such sickening back pain it left me wondering if I'd be fit enough to play in the Premier League. My post-match celebrations were cut short by a hospital date four days after Wembley to have the thumb joint put together again. It was a terrible mess. The surgeon had to make a cut on my right thumb and three further incisions in my forearm taking out sinews which they rapped around the joint to bind it together. That was the only option I had and the thumb still dislocates today. Thank God for being left handed!

Promotion was the perfect boost for my testimonial season which followed. A time when most people are winding down their careers, testimonials were rarities even back then, yet something I felt I deserved for my loyalty and commitment. There was a price for that loyalty. Because I was at Leicester for such a long time I didn't get the financial rewards of some of the other lads who came and went and won bigger contracts. I'm not complaining at all because it was still very good money and staying at Leicester was my choice. But my constant battles against injury were definitely a factor. I felt that, during those first ten years, I was constantly fighting for my future, worried my next deal would be my last. That never put me in a particularly good bargaining position to pin down a big contract like we went on to pay the other lads. Wages of £30k a week for Heskey, Izzet, Lennon and Elliott were unchartered waters for Leicester City making my maximum of £5k look like peanuts. But O'Neill judged contracts by the effort and commitment you put into playing and those lads never missed a game.

My testimonial season was a chance to meet fans who supported me so well over the years and also get some welcome money behind me. Infact it produced a good sum of £165.000 that enabled me to have a family house built at Skeffington. I was helped a great deal by David and Glynis Voss, who lived in the same village, and opened my testimonial events with a garden party. I knew the couple as David worked in finance. Glynis did an amazing job organising things very expertly behind the scenes for me .She also designed my house. I had been in rented properties for a while, notably in Barrow and Sileby, and the idea was to gain a pot of money and have our own house built which we did for £250,000. The 'if only' is that the same property is now worth £900,000 but the house was a casualty of my messy split and divorce from Debbie. I'm still bitter that a house I paid for from my testimonial could be taken away from me in court. I loved it there.

David Mellor, the former Home Secretary turned football pundit, who hosted Radio Five Live's 606 phone-in programme , spoke at one of my functions at Filbert Street although I'm not sure Martin was over keen on him! Generally, I had good support for my testimonial although there were times when Martin wasn't happy with my extra commitments. It all came to a head just after we lost 1-0 to West Ham United in the Premier League at Upton Park in October. As usual when we were in the capital, the manager, who lived in High Wycombe, was dropped off the coach at Waltham Abbey and in a terrible mood after we lost. It always took Martin a while to calm down and get defeat out of his system – like me - and a short coach journey was never going to be enough. He walked towards the back of the bus where I was sitting and made a very pointed remark about me being more interested in my testimonial than the team. I saw red, thinking his comment was well out of order. Stupidly, I followed Martin off the bus and demanded to know exactly what he meant. Things could easily have got more out of hand but he just blanked me and said he would see me at 9am on Monday.

I was wound up about the incident the whole weekend and there at Martin's office in good time to sort things out. Martin, being Martin, kept me waiting for about 90 minutes and still hadn't fully got over his disappointment from the West Ham game. The more we talked, the more we were falling out and, as he insulted me, we nearly came to blows. I got up to walk out before he suddenly said "Walshy, sit down" and started to relax again with me. We smoothed it over and shook hands. I could understand where he was coming from. A testimonial season involves a lot of events and it was in my nature to try to get to as many as I could to meet fans who had been so good to me over the years. Most functions were at night and were social occasions. It never occurred to me for one second, however, that my testimonial was more important than City's first season back in the Premier League. I don't think anyone who saw me play doubted my personal commitment during an historic, campaign for us. I'm sure, in the light of day, Martin didn't either. He was looking out for me at a very personally demanding time but let off steam after a below par City display. The important point was that, with O'Neill, we both had our say and moved on. He told me to inform him one week at a time how many events I was due to attend and I did just that. I went to a lot of working men's clubs, signed a lot of books and shared a lot of memories. But it never affected how I performed when I pulled on my blue Leicester City shirt and went out to battle. Infact, the warmth of support spurred me on.

As for the testimonial game itself, things didn't quite go to plan. It was a case of third time lucky – and third time unforgettable thanks to a certain Gazza and friends. Plan A was a clash between City and Aston Villa at the end of the 1996/97 season when we'd just won the League Cup. We planned to parade our hard earned cup in front of the fans to make it a double celebration and there couldn't have been too many more attractive visitors than Villa, still managed by Brian Little. Tension between him and City fans had died down now O'Neill was leading us to such successful times and he had no problem bringing a side to City to support me. The match would have been even tastier as Little had just signed a certain Stan Collymore for a cool £7m from Liverpool. A battle between me and Stan would definitely have been worth watching. Unfortunately Martin wasn't so keen. We had problems with the Filbert Street pitch towards the end of the campaign and the manager wanted the groundsman to get to work to ensure it was in better shape for the 1997/98 season. He told me not to worry because, if I waited a few more months, he could get a really big fish for me – he even joked about Barcelona. That was one promise Martin didn't live up to. Obviously he had thousands of things on his mind apart from my big game and left it a little too late. So to Plan C, a match between Leicester City and an All Stars side. The fans, all 16,000 of them, turned out in force for a great evening, both on and off the pitch.

Stars of the piece were Paul 'Gazza' Gascoigne and his celebrity DJ mate Chris Evans. They arrived together in style in a helicopter with Gazza clearly up for a good night. As we walked around the pitch before kick off, he offered me a coffee from his plastic cup. It turned out to be a cup full of whisky! Gazza enjoyed a sip or two before kick off yet the crowd would never have known as he still looked like a star. Gazza played the first half for City, managed by Brian Little, who true to his word returned to Filbert Street to back me. Fans may have thought it was part of a cunning plan that the former Spurs and England legend swapped shirts at half time and took his place among the All Stars for the second 45 minutes. That wasn't quite the case. He sat in the manager's room with his feet on his table smoking a cigarette and drinking whisky and was sent packing by Little. Testimonial, or no testimonial, he wasn't happy with Gazza's antics.

Afterwards, Evans invited me and my brother-in-law Neil to his room at the Grand Hotel where he was staying, saying he wanted 'a wedge'. Naturally I thought he meant some cash for his troubles. I was greeted by the DJ ordering three bottles of champagne. We sat on the bed having a drink when Evans showed us what he was talking about. He took a wedge out of his golf bag and started smashing golf balls around the hotel room. Sure, it was a bit strange but we were all in high spirits and no damage was done.

Then he suggested going to a night club and we ended up in the former Palais in Leicester. It was a Monday night and the place was rammed full of students in for a great surprise. Totally unannounced, Evans took over the venue and treated us all to a fantastic night. It was all spontaneous and great fun as the DJ bought everyone champagne. Liverpool legend John Barnes was the star attraction with the women while Gazza disappeared. When I went to breakfast at the Holiday Inn next morning, where my family had been staying, we found out Chris Evans had paid all our bills. Again, we had absolutely no idea he was going to do that. What a great bloke! He wasn't a bad footballer either by the way as he played in the match and even scored. Needless to say I was among the scorers, too, from the traditional penalty almost always awarded to the beneficiary on these occasions. Top referee Peter Jones, a big Leicester City fan, who wasn't able to officiate at our 'proper' matches, allowed me to re-take it when I blasted my first effort wide. I was never too clever at penalties. Just goes to prove I'm English!

Everyone has an opinion of Gazza. I was lucky enough to meet him that evening and see both sides – the incredibly talented footballer, one of the best England ever produced, and the self destructive alcoholic we worry about when we see photographs of him in the newspapers or on the TV. For me, he was top drawer that night. He was very hyper, that's for sure, but still entertained the crowd. He also gave me his Boro and Everton shirts when we played against each other. The reason we like him is that, deep down, Gazza just wants to please and be loved. It's sad what has happened to him and easy to understand how it has all come about. I've been close to that stage myself where it's possible to let yourself go and be lost to alcohol. Everyone is different. Whereas I make no secret of the fact that I have drunk to excess on many occasions, I'm not an alcoholic, nowhere near. I've always had a choice over how much I drink and, whilst writing this, have a grip on controlling my consumption. The reason is not because I am battling against the demons of drink but because I'm in control and can decide whether or not to drink. Alcoholics aren't that lucky. It is an addiction, an illness, and that's why we feel for a guy who is very unwell and just hope and pray he will get better.

WALSHY captained during my favourite ever Leicester City era; teams which played with style, versatility, flair and, thanks to Steve, aggression and steel. Every Leicester fan loves Walshy; few players have ever committed themselves so completely to one club and that kind of loyalty goes a long way with fans. When Walshy went up for a corner I'd shout from the old East Stand 'put my mortgage on Walshy!' Anyone who knows me will realise how much of a gamble that was but he rarely let me down. I've still got that bloody mortgage; sadly LCFC have no longer got Walshy leading the team.

I got to know Steve properly in 1990 when I sold his house in Burton-on-the-Wolds and have been lucky enough to remain mates since – he's written this book downstairs in my office over the last 12 months or so and he lights up our premises with his infectious and charming, yet shy, personality. No wonder he did so well with the ladies!

To whoever said you should never meet your heroes - allow me to introduce you to Steve Walsh.

Top bloke - top book - left wing, son!

NICK HUMPHREYS, friend, businessman and fellow fan

We may have been forgiven for worrying about how we'd do back in the Premier League, but there was a different feeling this time. We had a very good side in the making and, although the usual prophets of doom had us down for instant relegation, I genuinely thought we could surprise a few people. In the end, we did so well we even surprised ourselves!

O'Neill brought in good signings to add to the promotion squad. American Kasey Kellar took over the goalkeeper's jersey and we further bolstered the defence by adding Spencer Prior and Matt Elliott. The latter, in particular, was a massive signing for us and key to a lot that happened over the next few years. We often played a back three with me, as a left sided player, basically getting the role of a left back. After years of torture, I was well protected in that formation. We had Neil Lennon and Muzzy Izzet running miles up and down the field in front of us leaving me to bark out the orders. I was the voice of the side ensuring we kept our shape but not having to run around as much as in the past. No joking, those lads kept me going another five years. Another new signing later that season, Steve Guppy, was the teacher's pet. O'Neill had great faith in him and it was well rewarded. I constantly waved Guppy forward to do damage further up the field whilst I looked after his back. Having someone with his quality to supply crosses and set pieces made us a lot more dangerous in front of goal.

Up front we added another of the great characters of that O'Neill side, Ian Marshall. Signed from Ipswich Town for £800,000, Marshy was a Scouser who began his career with Everton but was every inch and curl a Tractor Man. With that mullet, he looked more like a farmer than a footballer and told us many times he never really wanted to be a professional player and only played for the money. He wasn't joking. He may not have been everyone's cup of tea and Premier League defenders weren't quaking in their boots when he joined us at Filbert Street but he was a typical O'Neill buy. Never very mobile, he limped rather than ran onto the pitch as a substitute and stood still a lot more than the rest of us. But we worked with what he was good at – and that was on the deck as well as in the air. Marshy unsettled defenders by winning more than his fair share of headers, even if his goal tally at Leicester owed much to me. I lost count of the number of knockdowns I made to allow Marshy to score especially in Madrid. But he repaid me with a few. Our finishing was always so lethal in training we were nicknamed smash 'n' grab by the lads as us oldies always beat the young ones in our Friday five-a-sides. Marshy became a real character in that City dressing room.

Kick off nearly never happened at all thanks to a bizarre incident before our opening match of the season at Sunderland. We were all ready for the start – apart from one thing. We hadn't signed our bonus sheets for performing in the top flight. The issue was mentioned on the team bus on the way to Sunderland and thrashed out there and then. Needless to say, canny O'Neill got the better of us. Although optimistic about our prospects, we were looking for a staying up bonus as that would be a massive achievement in itself; O'Neill was in favour of a staggered bonus for finishing in the top ten. Had we agreed, we would have all ended up a lot better off as we finished an amazing ninth. One guy who wasn't complaining was Pooley. He played a couple of games, let in three goals and netted a cool £96,000 bonus, more than the rest of the squad as he was always on the bench as a number two. Not bad business.

O'Neill was excited with a 0-0 draw to kick us off but, although we got our home show on the road with a 2-1 success in our midweek match against Southampton, we went on to make a slow start. We were beaten 2-0 at home by Arsenal before going down disappointingly at Hillsborough against Sheffield Wednesday and drawing 0-0 in our local derby at Forest. I've suffered a large number of injuries myself but on that day I saw one of the very worst. England midfielder Steve Stone collapsed right in front of me, clutching his knee. He had ruptured his patella tendon resulting in his knee cap rolling halfway up his thigh. I admit that was one of the few times in my long career when I almost felt physically sick. After Forest, we were well beaten on our own pitch 3-0 by Liverpool. We really got moving with a great 2-1 victory in a Sunday televised match against Tottenham Hotspur at White Hart Lane although it was a mixed afternoon for me – for more than one reason.

Spencer Prior's wife was the biggest flirt. She was mousy haired with a good figure but, in truth, not my type. Yet she made a bee line for me literally from the day her husband signed. We were playing golf at Park Hill club when I realised I'd forgotten my one wood. I didn't live too far away in Barrow and Mrs Prior volunteered enthusiastically to give me a lift home to fetch it. I didn't think too much of that but suddenly realised she wasn't driving me home at all. She took me down a dead end and parked up. We had a nice chat, I can tell you. It could have gone a lot further if she'd had her way. Enough said!

From then on, she made sure she was always around when the players' wives were invited to functions and came over to chat with me. I'm sure Spencer knew his wife was flirting with me and it was something that could easily get out of hand. At another function in Leicester, attended by my wife Debbie at the Holiday Inn, she joined in a game of spoof with the lads who all dropped out one by one leaving just the two of us. Mrs Prior suggested a forfeit for the loser of a sexual nature. Debbie understandably got the hump from watching us talking at the bar for so long. Nothing was ever going to happen in those circumstances but, again, I got the message.

It all came to a head when Mrs Prior rang my hotel room the night before the Spurs clash. I was sharing a room with Simon Grayson and Spencer was a few rooms away. I couldn't believe she was calling the night before a game. Larry witnessed the tone of the call and that I struggled to get her off the line. Again, there was no doubt what she wanted. Next morning Spencer had clearly been told about the phone call and was about to have a go when I turned the conversation around and said he needed to tell his wife not to ring me in future. The two of us handled the whole situation well and that was the end of the matter: she never phoned me again and kept her distance when I was around. Spencer and I often played together in the centre of City's defence and never let what happened affect our performances.

Back to the game itself, O'Neill asked before kick off who was on penalties. Nobody put their hands up to volunteer, so the boss looked at me and said I should take one, if it came our way. To be honest when the referee pointed to the spot in the second half, I'd totally forgotten! Nobody moved before I remembered what O'Neill had said. It must have taken me 10 minutes to walk from my defensive position to the penalty spot and I probably had too much time to think about it. I hit a very weak penalty that Ian Walker, later to become City's number one, got both hands to and half fumbled. I thought it had gone over the line but the cameras confirmed I was wrong. I was always prepared to put myself forward to take a kick in our shootouts but was never again even among the first five. Luckily, goals from Steve Claridge and Marshy ensured my miss wasn't costly against Spurs.

That win came either side of the two legs of our second round league cup tie with modest Scarborough. There were barely 4,000 people inside the Athletic Ground when we started a journey few imagined would lead to Wembley and even Europe. It was a potential banana skin against a Fourth Division side who would have loved to have put one over a Premier League outfit. Bet your life O'Neill saw the potential significance of it. He knew from his Forest days, where he picked up a couple of winners' medals under Cloughie, this was a competition in which the more modest top flight sides had a real chance. Big boys tended to neglect it with the teams they fielded but O'Neill was desperate to win every game we played. We won 2-0 that evening and 2-1 in the return at Filbert Street. Most memorable moment of the tie was poor Jamie Lawrence knocking himself out as he bravely scored one of our goals. That took us through to a very similar clash against York City at Bootham Crescent where goals from Neil Lennon and Simon Grayson took us through 2-0. Nobody outside Leicester batted an eyelid at those results but we were through to the last 16 of what we considered a major competition.

The Brian Little affair was still fresh enough in our minds for the league visit to Aston Villa to have even more spice than an average Midlands derby. Our boys were well up for it and won 3-1 thanks to Claridge, a Parker penalty and our Muzzy. I'm not exaggerating but honestly believe we even gave the great Fergie the shits. The great manager never enjoyed sending his great Manchester United side out to play us because he knew our style and that we'd always be strong physical opponents. That stemmed from the fourth round League Cup played in November at Filbert Street. With three other major competitions on his plate, including the Champions League, Fergie rested several star players. But one thing was absolutely certain: he thought he had enough in that dressing room to knock us out. Instead Steve Claridge and Emile Heskey scored the goals that gave us a famous 2-0 victory and helped our confidence no end.

Ironically, our first visit to Old Trafford under O'Neill came just a few days later. It was a game I remember more for what happened off rather than on the field. For some reason, O'Neill took us to Haydock Park Thistle hotel right across from the racecourse, to prepare. There were no big team talks or tactics just a training session on the racecourse the night before. All we did were a few under and overs like kids do. When we got back to the hotel, comedian Chubby Brown was a fellow guest. But even he got upstaged by our own joker Garry Parker. In the queue for food after training, John Robertson, O'Neill's assistant, was carrying two plates of food. He was dressed in his shorts when Parker sneaked up behind him and pulled them down. Like a true Scotsman, he was wearing nothing underneath. Parker was a great team mate, who livened up the dressing room with his practical jokes during the week and did the serious business on the pitch on a Saturday. His favourite party tricks included cutting the toes off my socks so I'd have a surprise when I came back into the dressing room. His pants stunt was just a bit more inconvenient; he rubbed deep heat into them so, on my way home, my bollocks were on fire! But he topped the lot when he took my keys and parked my car in Martin O'Neill's space. Needless to say that earned me a fine I knew very little about.

Another thing that settled us down before the game was a reunion with Keith Kent, then head groundsman at United. We loved Keith to bits but I have no idea how he got the job. When he was at City, he was largely a gardener who was with our laundry lady Sheila but pissed off to Manchester with her sister! The lads weren't too impressed with that because they loved our Sheila. Kenty wasn't known as an expert groundsman, to be honest, and it was no surprise to me the Old Trafford pitch was never as good as the team. Sharing a few memories with him on the pitch helped us feel a little more at home in what was a very intimidating occasion for most of us. There was definitely an aura about Manchester United and Old Trafford was one of the most frightening places to visit. On this occasion, there were more than 55,000 in the famous ground as United took revenge. Neil Lennon scored our goal in a 3-1 defeat.

WALSHY has to be one of my favourite City players. He was a bit reserved when he first came but, once he got his feet under the table, it was a different story. He became more friendly, more and more boisterous and the practical jokes got worse and worse. I can't publish some of the things he did because I don't want to spoil the book! He went through a lot of hard times including the injuries that lingered longer as he got older. I thought it was a real shame that Walshy left in the way he did and didn't become a club ambassador like Birch.

I've been a City fan since I was a 15 or 16-year-old schoolgirl and footballers never grow up; Birch has still got the mind of a teenager and I can't believe Walshy is about to turn 50 – he doesn't act like it! I'm pleased he's back around the club again and he always pops in when he wants something! Mind you, he buys me a box of Black Magic at Christmas, although he doesn't go to the same trouble as the man on the TV advert...you better get me a signed copy after this, Walshy!

SHEILA KENT, Leicester City laundry lady from 1978 to present day.

It was up and down stuff in the league, although we were doing more than enough to keep out of trouble. Christmas saw a Claridge goal nick us a very good point at Anfield before two days later we were disappointed to be held 2-2 by Forest, who were struggling at the bottom of the league. But come the New Year, the League Cup again gave us the morale boost we needed. Our quarter final trip to Ipswich Town was tense and difficult. We struggled for long spells that night at Portman Road and could easily have lost. Yet a late goal from Mark Robins left us dreaming of Wembley.

February brought a couple of remarkable games. Every time I came up against Newcastle things seemed to happen. Our latest trip to St James Park lived up to all expectations. It didn't seem to matter how many goals we scored against the Geordies, they always came back to beat us. Goals from Elliott, Claridge and Heskey saw us cruising at 3-1 with time fast running out. Then that warhorse Alan Shearer killed us as he inspired another great comeback. He almost burst the net from a free kick and ended up with a hat trick as we lost 4-3. Next up was Derby County at Filbert Street, the match that made Marshy a Foxes legend for life. Up to then we still hadn't beaten one of our main East Midlands rivals, having gone down 2-0 at Derby early in the season. But Marshy's never-to-be-forgotten hat trick settled that score as we won 4-2 in front of another big Filbert Street crowd.

It was perhaps the one disappointment of our great days under O'Neill that we didn't make a serious challenge in the FA Cup. There was no real reason for it as far as I could see. Yes, we targeted the League Cup in which we did so well but the manager was equally desperate for us to win whenever we went onto the pitch and would have loved to have led us to FA Cup glory as well. The nearest we came under Martin was in that same first season back in the Premier League after we had the good fortune of getting a couple of home draws in rounds three and four and seeing off Southend United and Norwich City. Next out the bag was a really big fish, Ruud Gullit's Chelsea, at Filbert Street on a cold Sunday afternoon. BBC TV cameras covered it as a live match, fully expecting their multi-talented line up, including brilliant Italian Gianfranco Zola, fresh from scoring the winner for Italy in the World Cup qualifier against England at Wembley, to sort out our patched up line up missing key players through both injury and suspension.

The tie looked to be slipping away from us when Roberto Di Matteo cut inside me to give Chelsea the lead, then Mark Hughes made it 2-0 before half time. Nobody expected us to come back, but we did. We always thought our best chance might come from set plays and that's how it turned out. Shortly after half time, Garry Parker floated over one of his teasing free kicks and, with goalkeeper Kevin Hitchcock a little slow to come off his line, I timed my leap perfectly to send a trademark header into the middle of the empty net. At 2-1 you're always in with a chance, but particularly Leicester City. We piled on the pressure towards the end until after 87 minutes we cracked them again. This time we had a bit of luck as Parker's lower free kick to the near post was turned into his own net by Eddie Newton. So we got a 2-2 draw and travelled to Stamford Bridge in good spirits for a fifth round replay.

That proved to be one of the most controversial nights of my Leicester career although, unusually, I didn't have too much to do with it. The match was very tight from beginning to end with nothing much to choose between the two sides. Then came an incident that had everyone talking about whether technology should be introduced to check penalty decisions. Norwegian Erland Johnsen went chasing into our penalty area where he basically collided with Spencer Prior. It wasn't a foul, definitely no peno, but the ref gave it. We were absolutely shattered. We'd done everything humanly possible to give us a chance of winning that tie and it was about to be ripped away from us by a rank bad decision. Up stepped that weasel Dennis Wise to twist the knife – or rather my nipples – as he came into the penalty area to have his say. Wise was perhaps the one player I never got full revenge on – and I owed him an even bigger one in another match for a terrible tackle on me which even had Sir Alex Ferguson raising his voice in disgust. But, on this occasion, the best I could do was slap him on the face – scant consolation for Frenchman Frank Le Boeuf sinking the penalty that knocked us out of the world's most famous cup competition.

There was a special 'Leicester' camaraderie when lads from different sports got together. Walshy, Nicco (Paul Nixon), James Whittaker, Deano (Dean Richards), Cockers (Richard Cockerill), Austin Healey, Westy (Dorian West) and I all had a regular post match Saturday night meet up for a few beers at Vin Quatres bar in King Street.

Watching Walshy play for the Foxes, I knew the qualities that made him a Filbert Street legend. It wasn't just his ability; it was his honesty and never-say-die attitude. He was a winner but also a fan. The rugby lads used to come down to the football to see some 'real' action and loved seeing Walshy get sent off!

I really enjoyed playing in five-a-side games with and against Walshy at the Goals Soccer Centre – luckily we never locked horns too closely because there would only have been one winner! Considering his physical approach, I'm sure he'd have been equally suited to rugby union had he not become a footballer.

Rules may be different, but we all share a lot in common – sheer hard work, pressure, injuries, incredible highs and lows. But it wasn't all 'shop' when we got together at Vin Quatres - we also got on famously well as people.

I'm really pleased to be writing about Walshy because he, like me, will always wear the public label of being a Leicester lad with great pride as we both led our sides into battle from the front. He gave so much to the Foxes during probably the most successful time in their history and he still roars them on from the stands as they compete with the best teams in the country today. Isn't it great to see the Foxes back where they belong!

'Team Leicestershire' will always be champions in my book and Walshy has written a damned big chapter in that story.

Cheers mate!

MARTIN JOHNSON OBE,
former Leicester Tigers and England rugby union legend.

The League Cup semi final draw against Wimbledon's Crazy Gang would have unsettled other teams – but not us. Managed by Joe Kinnear, Wimbledon had serious tough nuts in their dressing room including Vinny Jones and Mick Harford. They had good players but got where they did largely by intimidating teams. More talented opponents knew they were in for a physical fight when they played Wimbledon and some buckled. I think the whole of football owes Leicester City a big debt because we were the ones who put them in their place that season. I honestly believe that we broke Wimbledon and they were never the same again. We actually outfought them in every department, especially mine as I verbally and physically destroyed them.

It did us no harm at all that we went into that semi final having recently beaten Wimbledon 1-0 at Filbert Street in the league. But there wasn't much football played in the Filbert Street leg which finished 0-0. For some reason, there was a three-week gap between the first and second games, during which we went to Wimbledon and completed a league double with a 3-1 win. That would play on their minds for the cup tie as Leicester City weren't going to lie down. Yet we knew we were in for a hell of a physical and mental fight. They did anything possible, both within the rules and otherwise, to get in our faces and got away with murder on their own patch. No point moaning or sulking because we never expected much protection from the officials down there. It was a tight, nasty game with few clear chances, but the amount going on off the ball was almost unbelievable. Then Harford was brought on with about 15 minutes to go. I've met up with him a few times since and he's a nice guy to chat with but, on the field, he'd chat with you one moment and head-butt you off the ball the next. First thing he did was slap Matt Elliott on the face. The big man screamed at me in anger and frustration but I just laughed. Next it was my turn on the touchline as he punched me and should really have been sent off. Yet we held our nerve, fought fire with fire, and a Simon Grayson header was enough to take us to Wembley after a 1-1 draw after extra time. His celebration was one to remember too.

There was a drinking culture in our side. We were like a pub team, I used to say, but probably the best pub team ever. Martin was quite old fashioned in his outlook and saw the social side as good for our team spirit. We were usually sensible enough to drink at the right times and ensure it never affected our performances on the field. We, however, took things to another level in our preparations for the final after O'Neill took us away to Tenerife for a week as we had a fortnight's break between the 2-2 draw at Southampton and Wembley. I swear we never missed a night's drinking. How we got away with a 1-1 draw in the final at Wembley after all that I will never know.

Boro were full of foreign stars but no great shakes as a team. League matches between the two sides didn't give us too much of a clue – we won 2-0 at the Riverside Stadium and they returned the favour 3-1 at our place a few weeks before Wembley. Best known players in their ranks were Brazilians Juninho and

Emmerson and Italian 'silver fox' Fabrizio Ravanelli up front. From a City point of view, it's interesting to recall Nigel Pearson, now our manager, was at the heart of their defence. O'Neill played his hand by giving Swedish defender Pontus Kaamark a man-to-man marking job on Juninho which proved a genius tactic. There was never going to be a goal feast as I swear some of us used the 90 minutes plus extra time to sweat off our drinking from the previous week. I had a good game, restricting Ravanelli to two or three chances. He came with a big reputation but wasn't the most hard working of strikers, so I was always on his tail. Their biggest threat was probably Juninho running free with the ball but Kaamark did a really good job to ensure he was never given an inch.

Extra time was the last thing we wanted after our thirsty build up and, even worse, we went behind within five minutes. Lenny halted a run from Juninho but the ball fell to Ravanelli and this time he drove it into the back of the net. We were operating on empty but no way were we going to give in without a fight. Mark Robins came on as sub and I was pushed into attack for the closing stages. The switch brought us our reprieve with just a couple of minutes left. I got my head to a Robins cross to send it back across goal where Heskey headed against the bar. Claridge went in with several Boro defenders in the scramble for the loose ball and Heskey got the final touch to give us another chance.

What a relief that was to get away from Wembley without being beaten after our below par performance. Boro may have felt gutted at losing their lead so late but my thinking was clear; if we could hold them to a draw in the state we were in, only one team was going to win the replay at Hillsborough ten days later. I honestly felt that, after the disappointment of my earlier matches at the national stadium, I was now coming of age at Wembley as a player performing well on the biggest stage. I was very proud to win the Alan Hardaker Trophy for being man of the match.

The Hillsborough replay was one of the most memorable nights of my whole career as we lifted a major trophy for the first time in 33 years. We were feeling in better shape and, although we again needed Kaamark to do his special job on Juninho, always looked more likely to score than them. Best chance of the 90 minutes fell to Heskey who was denied by the woodwork for the second time in the tie. He struck his shot perfectly and it beat the goalkeeper only to rebound back into play off the inside of the post. That was bad luck but we still backed ourselves to win. I had Ravanelli well and truly in my pocket and he never had a kick. We were defending very comfortably and the only side who ever looked like breaking the deadlock. The golden moment came ten minutes into extra time. Garry Parker floated over a free kick from just inside the Boro half to the middle of the penalty area where I went up for the ball with Nigel Pearson. The incident has been much talked about considering Pearson's Leicester connections now but, honest Nigel, I didn't foul you. All I did was put my arm across him and head the ball back across goal for Claridge to steer his volley into the net. Dreamland, again!

We held out fairly comfortably for the next 20 minutes and we'd done it. I'd led City to victory and I added the Alan Hardaker Trophy for being best player over the two games to my winners' medal. This had to rank right up there with the Derby final. Lifting a major trophy in front of the Leicester faithful is better than larruping any woman! Honest. The rest of the night was a bit of a blur, although I didn't do too much drinking as I had taken extra strength or one too many Voltarol tablets - magnif they are. Getting up those steps to collect the trophy, one of the proudest moments of my life, was much more difficult than marking Ravanelli. There were so many celebrating City fans in the stand I could hardly find my way up the steps – at one stage I was going in the wrong direction! Birch led the drinking from the cup, along with Matty Elliott, who would drink anything, I can tell you. More surprisingly, Hesk, who usually didn't touch a drop of the hard stuff, joined in. Bad move, Bruno! On the coach on the way home, big Emile went to the toilet and was sick quite badly. He staggered out with his eyes rolling - I will never forget that look. He may have been nicknamed after the very popular boxer, but I swear he looked as white as a sheet, if that's possible. It was something of a joke to us in our excitable mood but not to his dad who came to collect him when we got back to Leicester. I tried my best to explain but he simply threw Emile's stuff into his car, followed by Emile on top, and sped into the night. The cup sustained quite a lot of damage as it was dropped and bashed around but we didn't care - it was ours, we owned it. We'd won a trophy and we were in Europe! Could it get any better?

Walshy on City's foreign legion: "Speaking the language, or having some understanding of it, is useful when foreign players join an English club but it didn't do too much harm for Theodoros Zagorakis, the captain of the Greek national team when they won Euro 2004, who was a more than useful member of Martin O'Neill's all-conquering side.

"Theo couldn't speak a word when he first came over but, for some reason, I understood him very well. He was a particularly good lad as well as being an outstanding midfielder who didn't quite get the credit he deserved despite taking part in League Cup finals against Tottenham and Tranmere Rovers.

"Top foreign player during my spell with City was undoubtedly the Swedish international Pontus Kamark. We were a very well organised defensive unit in those days but it was O'Neill's decision to use Pontus to man mark Juninho that won us the League Cup against Boro. As he showed for Atletico Madrid against us in the UEFA Cup, the Brazilian was one of the rare players with the natural ability to tear us apart, but Pontus did a fantastic job in both games to keep him quiet.

"Another import who made an immediate impression on me was the Finland striker Yari Rantanan, brought to the club by Hamilton after a poor start to the 1987-88 season. Yari didn't make too many appearances at Filbert Street but I will never forget seeing this guy, who looked like a Norse god, coming into a training game and immediately giving me the elbow.

That was never on and I soon made sure he was brought down to earth and he knew who I was for the rest of his shortish time in Leicester! They didn't mess with Walshy however big they were."

Not that O'Neill allowed us to think about that. Celebrations after the Boro game were long and hard but we still had the not-so-small matter of five more Premier League games to play. A funny story - although not at the time - came when we were 1-0 down at half time against Chelsea at Stamford Bridge less than 72 hours after winning the League Cup. O'Neill wasn't happy.

To make things much worse a mobile phone went off as he was about to lace into us. Mobiles were banned in the dressing room but this was no rebellion, just typical Steve Claridge. Never the most organised player with his kit, he left it switched on in his bag. O'Neill went crazy telling him to "turn that fucking phone off". It kept ringing and ringing. Steve tried and tried to find his phone, rummaging through his possessions and betting slips, before finally switching it off. I was caught up in the moment and couldn't help laughing my head off. That earned me a share of the fine O'Neill handed out for the striker's lack of discipline.

Although we didn't feel in any danger of relegation, we went into our home game against Manchester United two weeks later still needing three points to make absolutely certain of our place in the Premier League for the next season. That match provided me with another magical moment, leaving the great Dane Peter Schmeichel helpless from a corner – not from a header, but a half volley from inside the six yard box.

I still remind him of it when he comes to City matches to see his son Kasper keep goal for us and he laughs it off saying he can't remember. After knocking them out of the League Cup, we had them on the ropes again as Marshy scored a brilliant individual goal to put us 2-0 up inside 20 minutes. A young Ole Gunner Solksjaar partly ruined our day by saving a point for United with a couple of goals – but a 2-2 draw wasn't bad against a side who won the league by seven clear points.

A couple of victories over Sheffield Wednesday and Blackburn meant we finished in ninth spot with 47 points – a fantastic effort for a club of our size. We were ahead of massive clubs such as Spurs, Leeds and Everton, better off than Derby and, to the delight of Filbo fans, Forest finished bottom and were relegated. What a season!

The Blackburn victory was even more memorable for my night out with Larry at Simpkins night club on the eve of the game. We were still in party mood from our League Cup triumph and it was the only time in my career when I drank on a Friday night before a match – that's apart from when my Mum insisted I had a couple of small cans of Mackeson stout to get my iron levels up when I was at Wigan!

Helped by free drinks courtesy of Callum, son of good old Vince the owner – bless his soul – we had cocktails and champagne until late. If we'd had the League Cup with us, we'd have even drunk out of that! Staggering out of the club, as pissed as farts, you would never believe we had a game of top class football the following afternoon.

I've never been so pleased to look at a team sheet without my name on it as O'Neill, purely by co-incidence, rested me. I enjoyed it even more as Larry was in the starting eleven. Needless to say, he only lasted 30 minutes before being dragged off after having a shocker!

Walshy on international football: "I never thought I was good enough to be an international footballer, to be honest. I have always been an England fan, having lived through all their near misses and disappointments post 1966 and it would have been a fantastic honour to put on a Three Lions shirt.

"But the nearest I actually got to taking to the international stage was with Mick McCarthy's Republic of Ireland. Mick approached Martin O'Neill to say he was interested in including me in one of his squads if my links with Eire could be established. This was the way it worked: Mum spent about £300 going through my family history to see if I really did have Irish blood in me. Fair guess, I suppose, as Walsh is an Irish name. In the end, she went back far enough to find a link and I told McCarthy I was available as County Mayo in Westport was where my ancestory began. I love Ireland and have got some great friends over there, so this was exciting. Unfortunately, I then injured my knee and was out of action for a considerable period. The issue was never mentioned again."

Dreamland now!

Expression says it all. On the bench with Tater Peeler at Tranmere

Genius Martin O'Neill and his right hand man John Robertson

Ravanelli v Walsh tussle – Coca-Cola Cup Final Wembley

Take a look at Larry's suit!!

Loving the City away matches

Brian Little was a key part of my City success story

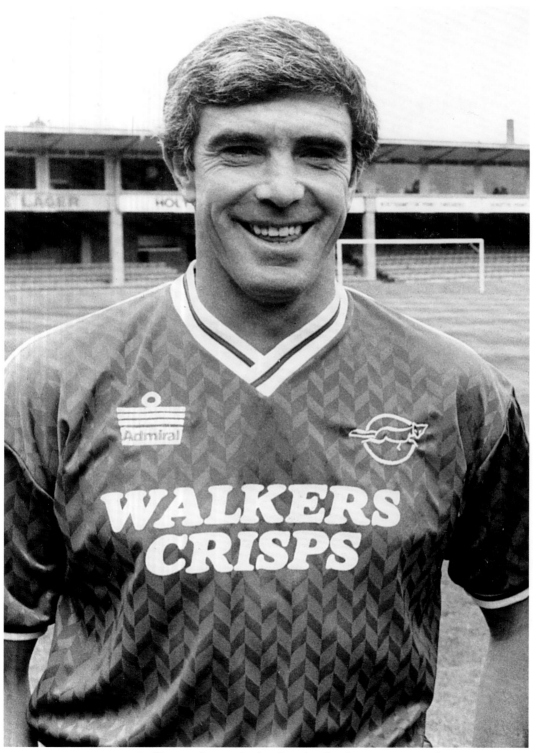

1986, a year I will never forget, signing for City, thanks to Bryan Hamilton

Hurting at Wembley

Captain Fantastic in action

Bust-up with Wrighty at Filbo

Walshy's mate the Birch MBE

Head to head with Bully

Chapter Seven

Into Europe and Out of the Door

I honestly thought I could become Leicester City's next manager

PLAYING in Europe was a dream but, typically, Martin O'Neill wanted more. Just as he was more concerned with finishing in the top half than escaping relegation, he wasn't going into Europe for the ride – he wanted to win it or, at least, have a great UEFA Cup run. He knew the impossible was possible after his days with Cloughie and wanted to taste the same glory as a manager himself. Even that wasn't all. The gaffer had his sights on bettering our ninth place finish and going all the way again in the League Cup. An FA Cup run would be nice, too, but he didn't want to be greedy!

With a massive European night against mighty Atletico Madrid on the horizon, we made a great start to the league. After seeing off Villa 1-0 on opening day – always good for Midlands pride – we went to Anfield and won 2-1. City had enjoyed some very good results against Liverpool in the past but to be a part of it was very, very special against a side including David James, Steve McManaman, Michael Owen and Paul Ince. Matty put us in front inside the opening 60 seconds and Graham Fenton made it 2-0 with seven minutes left. Ince pulled a goal back but we hung on to win.

We could so easily have made it a great Lancashire double the following weekend when Heskey tore apart Manchester United's defence in the opening minutes of our clash at Filbert Street. The big man could have had a hat trick early on and, although United had their share of chances afterwards, a 0-0 draw was another reminder that we really could compete with the very best.

Highlight of that interesting start to the season was Wednesday, August 27 and a totally unforgettable evening at home to Arsenal, who went on to become champions. I don't think anyone who was there will ever get bored at recounting what happened in one of the top five games of my career.

Hero of the night was Arsenal's Dennis Bergkamp who had to be one of the best strikers – if not the best – I ever played against. He was world class; his movement and awareness were incredible. Sometimes you can tell when a great player is on his game and the Dutchman was zoned in from the beginning, making very good runs and looking particularly sharp. That prompted me to take action. Bergkamp started on my side of the pitch until I gave him a (friendly) butt on the back of the head. That prompted him to stare at me then piss off to Matt Elliott's side which was good for me! The magical striker got the only goal of the first half with a cracking long shot but the fireworks really started after the break.

When Bergkamp produced a lightening turn to leave us for dead and chip the Gunners into a 2-0 lead, it looked like game over. Against almost any other side in the Premier League, it would have been. But Foxes never die. We don't feel sorry for ourselves and quit, we dig deep. There were six or seven minutes left when Hesk scrambled a goal from close range to give us hope. We knew we could throw the kitchen sink at Arsenal or, more accurately, the full force of Elliott and Walsh, as the big men joined the attack.

The last few minutes were magical mayhem. The sight of Elliott suddenly appearing in the left wing position, cutting inside and leaving David Seaman helpless with a low shot would have sent most of our fans home more than happy. But the drama just kept on happening as we went into injury time. Bergkamp's third goal was one of the best I ever witnessed on a football pitch. He took a long ball forward out of the air, turned in the same sweet movement and, almost casually, flicked it into the net. My only consolation was he took Elliott out of the game instead of me. Surely it was all over this time? But we broke forward to win one last corner. Garry Parker swung it over and folklore has it that we played a game of head tennis in the Arsenal area. It wasn't quite like that as I'm sure my defensive partner Spencer Prior was aiming to score himself when he nodded across goal and straight onto my head. I sent the ball crashing into the roof of the net and set off on one of the celebrations of my life.

I've got sympathy with goalscorers who go over the top when they score and celebrate in front of the opposition fans because, for a few short seconds, you haven't got a clue what you're doing. It's the most unbelievable feeling in the world, like going into oblivion. I headed straight towards the Arsenal bench to make sure Wrighty hadn't missed it and told him so. We'd had a verbal and physical tussle all evening until Wrighty had been substituted with manager Arsene Wenger thinking the points were safe. The final whistle went a few seconds later and players and officials from both sides poured onto the pitch with Wrighty bent on revenge. I was telling him I was up for a fight and was so wide-eyed and excitable anything was possible. I wanted to fight anyone who fancied it. For all of you dying to know, what I said to him was "come on, Wrighty, let's have it!" The rest of the lads did their best to separate us as we came off the pitch before we continued firing off at each other in the tunnel. Then the handbags were put away.

A few days later we were both ordered by the FA to attend a special disciplinary hearing at Lancaster Gate. Tells you loads about the two sides that, as I arrived with Martin O'Neill after coming down on the train, Wrighty was lauding it in a chauffeur-driven car. Our argument, however, was settled before the masters at the FA got down to business. Wrighty had a word in my ear going up the steps suggesting we put it all down to a bit of a wind up and promised to send me a signed shirt as a gesture of thanks. I agreed. The panel decided on no further action and the shirt arrived a couple of days later! Still got it today – Wrighty, top man!

We set off for Madrid on the back of another victory over Spurs and another confidence boost for me. It wasn't until the second half that we opened the scoring in a 3-0 win, but it was worth the wait. Parker swung over a free kick that was just perfect for me to jump at the far post and head back across Ian Walker. Great feeling.

There was a big build up to the first leg of the UEFA Cup tie in Madrid with a lot of talk about whether we could again stop Juninho, who had moved to Spain for £12m after we'd got the better of him at Boro. But he was far from the only top name in that side. There was Spanish striker Kiko, who wasn't too hard to locate on the pitch as he whistled constantly which reminded me where he was. He didn't enjoy some of my challenges on the night, but they were nothing compared with the stick Daniel Prodan handed out to Marshy and Heskey - wish I'd been up front to sort the fucker out! Christian Vieri, their 10 million Euros top goalscorer at The Calderon, was another big threat.

The talking did nothing to prepare me for that moment walking out of the tunnel into an electric atmosphere with red flares and fire everywhere I looked. As you know, I wasn't easily scared on a football pitch but that took my breath away.

Just for a moment I wondered what on earth I was doing there. Then it was on with the task in hand: I said to the lads "this is it, boys, let's get fired into them, we will take these, don't you worry." The Blue Army numbered 3,000 in that great stadium – they came by plane, coach and boats on what for many was a very difficult trip, defying a number of well-publicised hitches in the arrangements. They were thrilled as we took the lead after just 11 minutes. What surprised me most was just how simple it was. I had yards of space at the far post to head Parker's chip down and back across the box for Marshy to sweep the ball in from close range. If we could do that once, why not two or three times? Unfortunately, it didn't turn out that way. But that famous photo of Marshy, my smash 'n' grab mate was very special! Just a shame I wasn't on it after my assist.

O'Neill's tactic of man marking Juninho with Kaamark was working again as we managed to restrict him in the first half to set pieces. But things were beginning to turn against us. Marshy was injured after a very heavy tackle and had to be replaced by Claridge and, unknown to everyone else, I was soon carrying an injury too. I felt my hamstring go just before the half hour. It wasn't fully torn but I knew I'd done something bad. I never said anything because the last thing I wanted was to come off early. It was an amazing historical night and we fight to the death. We had one golden chance to really take control by making it 2-0. Soon after coming on, Claridge lobbed the ball over the goalkeeper but onto the roof of the net. Had he been on the pitch for longer, who knows?

I soldiered through the 90 minutes without further injury worries but the game became harder and harder. To their credit, Atletico started to create more openings only for Kasey Kellar to deny them before Juninho produced a blistering move with Kiko to level the scores with a deflected shot. We needed to calm things down for a few minutes as a volatile home crowd got behind Atletico – instead the referee made things worse. To say the penalty award, against Steve Guppy for an innocuous challenge on Delfi Gelli just inside the area, was dubious is being kind. Away teams don't tend to get the rub of the green decision-wise in Europe but we were convinced there was more to it. For all sorts of reasons, certain people wanted to see Atletico progress in Europe rather than the relatively unknown Leicester City and O'Neill and our lads were left steaming at the injustice of it after the final whistle. It could easily have been far worse for me however. The red mist came down when the spot kick was awarded and we made sure Gelli knew exactly what we thought. That was no excuse, however, for me blatantly head-butting Kiko but he was stirring it. That was another one I got away with. He went mental trying to attract the referee's attention as an awful thought went through my head: was I going to be sent off on one of the biggest nights in City's history? But none of the officials saw it. There were scuffles between both sets of players and the bad feeling continued throughout the tie. Vieri slotted the penalty to give Atletico a 2-1 win on the night. But we had an important away goal and this tie was in the balance. I fancied us at Filbo big time.

Most of the City lads went out that night but I stayed in the hotel, not wanting to push my luck any further after the Kiko incident. I was also struggling with my hammy and the tablets which always affected my stomach. I had got away with it on the pitch but, knowing the Atletico lads were going to the same night club, I fancied I was better off having a quiet one. I had a few drinks with some City staff whilst the lads rolled in about 4am. Apparently I missed a massive night, so I ended up sorry. With not too many thoughts about getting our heads down for the weekend trip to Elland Road, the lads partied, as we did back then, late into the morning. It felt like we had won!

With our away goal in the bag, we knew we could squeeze through with just a 1-0 victory in the return leg at Filbert Street but again things didn't turn out as expected for either me or the team. Knowing I'd tweaked a hamstring in Madrid, I didn't train too much in the days after the tie but was in the side that went to Leeds United on the Saturday, a match that's always a scrap. That should have been a very happy day for me. I scored the winning goal in a 1-0 success at Elland Road – another great result. But I ripped the hamstring and had to limp off shortly after getting the winner just before half time. Even more seriously that meant a six-week lay off and no chance of playing in the second leg of the European tie, I was devastated as I knew the lads needed me.

Any suspicions we had about the refereeing from the first leg were multiplied tenfold by what happened back in Leicester. I never enjoyed watching the games when I was injured, but that match against Atletico was one of the most frustrating 90 minutes ever. That was O'Neill's big mission to do well in Europe and I'm convinced we could have done so given better officiating. I was also bitterly disappointed not to get another chance to play myself. I knew I could have had Kiko in my pocket for another 90 minutes and get more chances to cause problems at set pieces, which appeared to be Madrid's weakness. The first half was tight and the scores remained 2-1 on aggregate at the interval. The game started to open up in the second half, especially when the referee became card-happy. Juan Lopez was sent off near the hour mark after a heavy challenge on Emile and we began to take control. A few minutes later, the referee sent off Garry Parker in one of the worst decisions I have seen. Garry, already booked, took a quick free-kick on the edge of the box before the whistle was blown. Somehow the ref gave Garry a second yellow and we were down to ten men as well. This cost us the tie as it had been only a matter of time before our dominance turned into goals. Instead Garry's sending-off handed the initiative back to Atletico, who exploited the extra space. Juninho, let loose by Kaamark now, scored their first with about 20 minutes remaining before setting up my mate Kiko, who sealed the tie a few minutes later. It was a great effort from the lads in both legs against a massive club and further helped to put our name on the map. There can't have been too many hard feelings from Atletico as both Vieiri and Kiko gave me their shirts from the second leg. Our European adventure was over after just one tie, but we had enjoyed a taste of the big time and were determined to make an impact in the Premier League again that season.

Martin, being Martin, was probably just as upset with our League Cup exit a few weeks later. And, for me, that defeat was definitely more physically painful. Talk about coming down to earth as we were humbled 3-1 by Grimsby Town at Blundell Park. I was one of two players injured trying to prevent one of the goals. Richard Smith and I both made desperate attempts to clear a ball off the line.

He collided with our goalkeeper and needed stitches to his head but I came off even worse. I smacked straight into a goalpost and broke my ribs. Breaking your leg is painful, believe me, but nothing compared with that. It didn't help that, for some minutes, Richard was attended to whilst I lay there gasping for breath. We were both taken to hospital and it took me eight weeks to fully recover. Even the fish and chips tasted shit that night! That proved to be a disappointing cup campaign all round as we also went out of the FA Cup too early for our liking, beaten 3-0 in the fourth round at Crystal Palace.

I was in Baffone restaurant, a popular haunt of the players I'd introduced Steve to run by the godfather (Pepe) and Sal, one lunchtime with Steve, Neil Lennon, and Simon Grayson, who had been recently transferred to Villa. Steve and Neil jokingly said to Larry 'we will get you in the early minutes of the game' between the two sides at Villa Park.

The game kicked off, and to the amazement of our away support, but not me, they did! I remember Lenny chasing Larry down from the kick off and cleaning him out. I loved it but I'm not sure it was in Martin's game plan!

Incredibly on the M6 travelling to that game, the team bus was in front of me and I jokingly rang Steve and asked if he would fix my settee (remembering his upholstery background from years before).

Such a great guy, he said he would but he had to beat Villa first...!

By KEVIN BOURGAULT, massive City fan and close mate

Our highlights were therefore in the Premier League on our way to another great finish of 10th place. Adding to Fergie's fears about us by actually going to Old Trafford and beating Manchester United was a fantastic achievement. Tony Cottee scored a goal that became very important come the end of the season when United were denied the title by a single point. I came off injured after having a great game during that memorable 90 minutes but there was no end to the joy in the Cottee family – as TC's dad had a cheeky £20 bet on his son scoring the first goal at 25-1 and landed himself a cool £500 profit.

For the fans, however, being 4-0 up at Pride Park inside 15 minutes against local rivals Derby took some beating. That was a Sunday afternoon when we stormed The Rams with an aerial bombardment - all four of our early goals came from headers without me getting in on the act. Hesk was on fire, helping himself to a couple. I swear that was the best short spell of football I was ever involved in – and the fact it was against Derby made it even sweeter. Dean Sturridge, who had given me the big one, got verbally hounded by me and stayed well away. One of my main memories was typical O'Neill as we came into the dressing room at half time in great spirits. He gave us a verbal lashing to ensure we weren't complacent in the second half.

Walshy on City's biggest rivals: "Ask the notorious Baby Squad boys, who took on the hardest fans throughout the country, and there was no doubt who they hated most – Nottingham Forest. Look at the map and you could make out a case that Coventry City, a few miles up the M69, were our chief enemy, yet the Sky Blues weren't top of my hate list.

"The truth is that all the Midlands derbies were very big games. Whether it was Forest, Cov, Brum or Villa, they were always huge occasions, ones I looked forward to as soon as the season's fixtures came out. Funnily enough, I always got on pretty well with the Forest lads – Marlon Harewood and Pierre van Hooijdonk apart – and our biggest rivals in my mind were always Derby County. There was extra feeling between the players when we played Derby, particularly on their home soil. It wasn't just the fouls, but niggly things when the ball went out of play such as fans waiting for us to collect the ball, then throwing it in our faces. Once at Filbert Street against Derby, I got reported to the FA – and fined – for throwing the ball back at a Rams fan and sticking up a V sign. At the hearing, I told them the fingers were saluting the two goals I scored against them at Wembley – unfortunately, it didn't quite add up in their minds.

"One game at Filbo, I was suspended and watching alongside my good mate Smudger when Mark Pembridge committed a shocking foul on David Oldfield that resulted in one of the worst cuts I've ever seen – it was like a shark bite on his calf. It was that bad I came down from the stand at half time to the tunnel area and gave him a whack around the head telling him he was bang out of order. Everything then kicked off between me and the Derby players.

"I'd also have to mention Wolves, mostly because of my long running battle with Steve Bull. We took turns to take pieces out of each other and both got ourselves into plenty of trouble doing so. The difference is I look back on those times with extra pleasure now because we've since been able to laugh about what happened and there's a healthy feeling of mutual respect there. But, let's be honest, I'd still like to kick him."

Our third season back in the Premier League began with a game given even higher profile as it was David Beckham's first after his sending off against Argentina in the 1998 World Cup. Many people across the country turned against Becks after that incident but he was still a hero in Manchester and played a major role in denying us another famous victory. It was an honour for me to walk out of the tunnel as skipper of Leicester City alongside one of the country's best players.

Talk about Fergie time it must have been the 185th minute when the England star curled a great free kick into the bottom corner of substitute goalkeeper Peggy Arphexad's net to earn United a last gasp 2-2 draw. United scored a hell of a lot of goals in added time but we felt we'd done enough to win it before then. Before the game O'Neill started to read out the United team in the dressing room – he stopped instead to read out the substitutes Giggs, Scholes, Sheringham and co. "If that's not enough to frighten you, nothing will; now go out and beat the bastards!" gaffer said. We knew what we were capable of after our great performances against them in the previous two seasons. We were in dreamland when Heskey and Tony Cottee scored to put us 2-0 up and were playing some great football to stun a crowd of 55,000. There really didn't look any way back for United but things started to turn against us. First goalkeeper Kasey Kellar went off with a knee injury on the hour after a challenge with Andy Cole, then Matt Elliott suffered a broken nose and came off - there's no way I would have done! Sheringham came on for Gary Neville and did my mate Muzzy on the touchline with a definite foul. He got away with it so they pulled one back with 12 minutes to go. Sheringham then got a taste of his own medicine when my head collided with his face and we had a face off head- to-head - he knew he was in a game now! But Fergie time came to the rescue, like so many times when referees melted and kept the match going when it should have been over. Step up David Beckham to spare Man U's blushes.

We were absolutely gutted in the dressing room afterwards as if we had been well beaten only for O'Neill to show us what a great manager he was. He chose that moment of despair to lift every player's spirits by reminding us how well we'd played and that he'd never swap any of our players for those in Fergie's dressing room. He could see we were battered and bruised and had run out of luck when we needed it most. That was the Manchester United side that went on to win the famous treble – the league title, FA Cup and Champions League when they left it almost as late as against us before beating Bayern Munich. Being disappointed with a draw at the Theatre of Dreams was also a reality check for me to show how far the Foxes had come since being promoted.

The following Saturday wasn't too bad either as we beat Everton 2-0 at Filbert Street before suffering a difficult spell. O'Neill kept refuelling our belief that we were good enough and we always bounced back. There was no slipping up on the League Cup banana skin as we saw off Chesterfield 6-1 on aggregate before another priceless Cottee winner got us back on track in the league with a 1-0 success against Leeds United at Elland Road. Leeds were also important in our latest League Cup run as we saw off the Yorkshire side, Charlton Athletic and Blackburn Rovers by the odd goal to send us into Christmas believing we had a chance of another return to Wembley.

We were doing pretty well in the league, too, with Liverpool beaten again by a single goal at Filbo and a popular win just before the festive season when we came back from a goal down to beat struggling Forest 3-1. To make the day even better for our supporters, they had their controversial Dutch striker Pierre van Hooijdonk sent off in the second half. I laid into him big time until he had enough and fell into my plan. Forest took an early lead in that game as Harewood skinned me to break free and finish. There was no way he was going do that again so I got in his face. From that moment, I tortured him verbally and physically and he never had another sniff.

Manchester United brought us temporarily crashing back down to earth when they thrashed us 6-2 at Filbert Street, showing the form that took them to their historic treble. Strikers Dwight Yorke and Andy Cole ran riot that afternoon which wasn't good news for me as a centre half. Yorke got a hat trick and Cole two and even the goal I scored in reply earned me more ribbing than congratulations. It was one of the strangest of my career as Guppy's close range shot hit me and rebounded into the net. Strangely enough, that's the one Peter Schmeichel prefers to talk about when he sees me.

The FA Cup again didn't really happen for us that season. We saw off Birmingham City 4-2 in the third round at Filbert Street before being convincing beaten 3-0 at home by local rivals Coventry City. No good for M69 bragging rights! That made it even more vital we put in a good performance in the League Cup against Sunderland. You usually bet on a semi final tie being a very close affair and our two legs against the Weirsiders didn't disappoint.

That was a tie Tony Cottee will never forget as he scored all three goals that eventually edged us through to Wembley. There weren't too many better examples of the manager's nouse in the transfer market than when he bought Cottee back to England from a club in Malaysia in August 1997. The guy is a huge West Ham legend who wrote himself into East End hearts with his instinct for goalscoring in two spells, with a very successful spell at Everton in-between. But most folk wrote him off when he disappeared to the Far East. Not too many top flight managers would have gambled on nursing him back to full match fitness and produce what he did. He had a loan spell at Birmingham City during his first season with us but it was during the 1998/99 season – and the Sunderland tie in particular – when he showed just what a good judge of a player and a character Martin O'Neill was. The deal clincher in many ways was that Cottee was still hungry. He had nothing to prove as a striker who'd bagged nearly 300 career goals but still didn't have a winner's medal in league or cup to hang around his neck. Thanks to O'Neill and Leicester City, he put that right during his successful spell with us. TC was almost a born again striker. He was rejuvenated after drifting out of the English game and top class football.

TC was a great lad who fitted in very well with us from the start, being part of the banter involving Marshy, Gary Parker and me to name just three. He became part of the togetherness of that side and was a natural goalscorer. You can buy such talent, but never teach it. It's more about instinct. TC knew where to go to get on the end of moves and find that half a yard of space you need to score a goal. I'm not being arrogant but it was something I recognised because I had it too. Some of it came from being a defender myself and getting to know the movement of the best strikers; the rest was pure instinct. Whenever you saw a player such as TC or Gary Lineker tap the ball into the net from a few yards out, it was rarely just good luck - they were lethal. Being in the right place at the right time is an art form.

The atmosphere at the Stadium of Light for the first leg was cracking, as it always is at Sunderland. It was going to take big men to stand up to those expectations but we had plenty. Talking of big men, Niall Quinn, fluffed an early chance to put the home side ahead but when a chance came his way Cottee was razor sharp. The dancing feet of Frank Sinclair down the right provided just half a chance and TC got across his man at the near post to flick us into an all-important lead. We were well on top and doubled our advantage in the second half and again it was Cottee who pounced on a loose ball and drilled it into the corner of the net from just outside the box. We were disappointed to concede a sloppy goal direct from a free kick towards the end to ensure there was no complacency when we kicked off back at Filbert Street for the decisive second leg.

Starting with a lead is difficult sometimes and it was Sunderland who had to come at us in the first half as we looked nervy and tentative. Quinn had already missed one great chance before he nodded a ball past Kasey Kellar and we were back level at 2-2 on aggregate. Now it really was game on! O'Neill, rightly, had a real pop at us at half time. He could see we needed to assert ourselves quickly or our hopes of winning the Worthington Cup would be over. We did just that. If the first half was Sunderland's, there's no doubt we bossed the second. Cottee's winner was, in some ways, a repeat of his first goal at Sunderland. Again he was quickest to react in the Sunderland box and sent a great flick past the goalkeeper to put us back in front overall. Kellar made one great save towards the end, but we'd done it – and deservedly so.

Just three days later we experienced the other side of the footballing coin - thrashed 5-0 by Arsenal at Highbury. It was a weakened City side with Hesk and TC both injured and me on the bench after being knackered in midweek. There was never a better example of how difficult we found it playing the Gunners on their own patch as they destroyed us in the first half. A young version of the incredible sulk,

Nikola Anelka, helped himself to a hat trick as the points were well and truly lost as we trailed 4-0. But the man who really shone yet again was Dennis Bergkamp. If anything he was even sharper than in the previous season's game at Filbert Street as he set up three of the first four goals – and added another assist for two-goal Ray Parlour just three minutes after the break.

Usually when you're a substitute, you're in the manager's ear urging him to get you onto the pitch. That day was just the opposite. Marshy and I agreed there was no way we wanted to come on in the second half as there was nothing to gain. Marshy didn't even bother to warm up once but I got the dreaded call from O'Neill as he sent on Andy Impey and me at the interval to try to galvanise us, much to Marshy's amusement. Matt Elliott wasn't complaining as the manager pushed him up front – safely away from his tormentor. Arsenal dominated the whole match but a combination of good goalkeeping by Kasey Keller and a series of narrow misses prevented them from adding to their already huge margin.

At the final whistle, I instinctively asked Bergkamp to swap shirts and he agreed, but said he didn't want mine! I guess I could understand: he has world class players in his collection, why would he want a Walshy shirt for his living room? I was more relieved at not having to reveal my physique to the TV cameras than offended by the Dutchman's attitude. But O'Neill wasn't happy. He went ballistic saying we'd just got thrashed and all I was interested in was getting an opponent's shirt. It didn't impress him either when I pointed out we'd only lost 1-0 whilst I was on the pitch! I could understand the manager's anger. He didn't want us to be in awe of anyone – even the world class Bergkamp – because we were proving week by week we could live with the best. That wasn't the point. I never gave any less than 100 per cent whoever I was playing against and it was no crime to get a cherished memento from a player who was always different class whenever we played against him. I just don't show the shirt to Martin when he comes round to visit! Bergkamp gave me three shirts in total even though I butted him - must be a quick forgiver as well as a fantastic player!

We weren't in the best Premier League form before the League Cup final against Spurs and relieved to break our duck for 1999 with a 1-0 success at Wimbledon a couple of games before Wembley to boost our confidence for the big day. I still ask myself how we lost that League Cup final to Spurs. It should never have happened. That was the cup final in which some of our lads - Tony Cottee and Frank Sinclair included – were investigated for the sale of tickets. The usual way of things was that players would get about ten tickets for the cup final and some from Cottee and

Sinclair appeared to get into the wrong hands of Spurs fans which caused several serious incidents. To make things even worse for Frankie, he was also dropped from the cup final side after breaking O'Neill's curfew by leaving the hotel the night before the game.

As for me, I always needed loads of tickets and actually asked for more than my original allocation. I got hold of about 150 in all and needed them all for a massive following of mates and family, so great was the interest in the match. Normally for a league match you got two tickets each handed out by the captain; not everyone wanted them, especially new signings. So, if you were on the ball, you got in there first and asked them for theirs. I always needed double figures every game and the lads were pretty kind to me as I had been at City a lifetime. But, as the games got bigger, the lads started to need them, so it became very difficult. Away games were dangerous as many a time my Dad's tickets were stolen by Ant Reid who would go to the players' entrance and say two tickets had been left by Steve Walsh for him. Nine times out of ten he was in and Dad had to blag some more! Good old Reidy, I'll get you back one day!

That final was one of my biggest disappointments in a City shirt. Both the team and particularly O'Neill were left fuming because we knew we should have won. My preparation could have been better as I was going through a bad time at home and taking any chance to stay out with the lads and drink in excess. It wasn't a classic football match by any means but the few chances created during the 90 minutes came our way. Hesk was denied by a last ditch tackle by Ramon Vega after being chipped through the centre by Robbie Savage in the first half but the closest we came was when Ian Walker parried a good shot from our defender Rob Ullathorne in the second period and then reacted very quickly when Cottee was set to snaffle the rebound. The game swung even more in our favour in the 63rd minute when Spurs went down to ten men. You don't need me to tell you that Savage got up people's noses on so many occasions and this one should have worked much to our advantage. He wrestled Edinburgh down near the halfway line and the Spurs man lost it, swinging his arm and catching Savage on the head. It was yellow for Savage and red for Edinburgh, who became one of the few players to get sent off in a major Wembley final. I immediately felt 'this is it we are gonna win this game now' as we were in full control.

From a Spurs free kick we never even set up. We switched off and got caught down our left side. I was guilty and that one moment of poor concentration cost us. Darren Anderton, who had a quiet game, slipped the ball to Les Ferdinand who found Stefan Iverson racing down the left side of our defence, the area I was defending. For the only time in the game really I let my guard slip and how we paid for it. I thought I had Iverson covered no problem but his cross from a tight angle was parried by Kasey Kellar straight into the path of the diving Alan Neilson, who headed into the empty net. There was no earthly way back after that. Our chance had gone. O'Neill was completely gutted afterwards but we didn't need telling we shouldn't have lost. The fact that we beat Tottenham 2-0 at White Hart Lane in our next league game to complete the double over them was good, but painful at the same time – we knew we were better than Spurs and should have won the silverware to prove it. Instead runners up medals were all we had to show. Altogether we enjoyed a good end to the league season which saw us finish 10th. Blue eyed boy Gupps scored a great goal at Chelsea in a 2-2 draw.

I first met Walshy at Glen Gorse Golf when we were both coming towards the most successful parts of our careers and he was a big athletic guy full of fun and laughter.

The links between the football and cricket clubs were very strong in the 1990s, helped by the fact that Martin O'Neill loved his cricket. We were all very proud to be part of a great time in Leicestershire sport – Tigers always seemed to be top of the tree but, for us and the football lads, it was a lot about team spirit and producing at an elite level, without always having a large number of top class individuals.

We shared a lot in common because there are a lot of similarities. We were both lads who moved to Leicestershire, took the place to heart as our second home and have always wanted to be a part of it. On the field, we both knew all about one or two-year contracts and the reality that you are only a couple of poor seasons from being out the door.

Professional sport, however successful you are, involves more lows than highs and training than match days plus, of course, the pain of getting yourself back from injury and onto the field.

I was told when I was about 30 my knees probably wouldn't take keeping wicket any longer yet battled on just as Walshy continually dragged himself onto the pitch to play for City.

I know how hard it is for players, particularly when they have been the centre of attention at their club for so long, when it all ends. Thankfully the cricket authorities as well as the PFA are doing more now to prepare today's players for that shock to the system.

I'm club ambassador at the County now and Walshy once again has strong links with City. We also are involved in a great education academy initiative to develop stars of the future in our respective sports.

PAUL 'NICCO' NIXON, former Leicestershire and England cricketer

I suffered a very strange injury on the first day of 1999-2000 season at Arsenal. I was really fit after going through a hard pre-season and came through all the friendly matches fully fit going to Highbury, where I can barely remember getting a point. We played really well and only went down 2-1 but it turned into a disastrous afternoon nevertheless as both Emile Heskey and I were stretchered off before the break. I was on the halfway line when I turned very innocuously, resulting in a badly torn abductor muscle that pulled a piece of bone from my pelvis. There is a hollow side now in my leg where the muscle has disappeared. It was a strange injury, causing the medics to not really know how long I'd be out of action and plunging me into a downer which had disastrous consequences. I was sat in the dressing room waiting for the lads to finish just listening for any goals. We took the lead in the 57th minute through Tony Cottee only for that man Bergkamp to equalise for the Gunners midway through the second half. Then it was time for Frank Sinclair to do his party trick. He'd started to get a reputation for not only being an outstanding defender but also scoring own goals and he couldn't have timed this one worse as he handed Arsenal a 2-1 victory in the 90th minute. None of us could believe it when just two games later we were leading mighty Chelsea 2-1 going into the last minute and Frank went and did it again to force a 2-2 draw. I got a taste that slowly things were coming to an end at City that season as I made only 10 starts and eight substitute appearances. It meant handing over the coveted armband for much of the season to my defensive colleague Matt Elliott. It was the sign of things to come for me as off the field events started to spiral down a slippery road.

On the Monday evening I had a scan and my fears were confirmed: I was out for a lengthy period. Still trying to come to terms with my latest setback, I went out with drinking partner Peter Welsh to The Cradock Arms, a local pub we regularly went to. This was one of those nights when best intentions went out of the window. We got there about 6pm and, once I'd had a few, I did the right thing, for once, and handed my car keys to the guy behind the bar to remind myself it's not the right thing to drink and drive and think instead of the safety of others.

I can't say I hadn't been warned. I'd driven over the alcohol limit many times and got away with it. I actually believed I was a better driver - how stupid! It was as if I didn't care about anyone else; like a lot of footballers, I was in my own world back then and nothing really bothered me. But one particularly near miss shook me up. I was in my BMW coming back home at about midnight from a night with another woman and had been drinking. I was driving fast along a country road in Stoughton heading back to Skeffington when I lost control of the vehicle going over a bridge. The vehicle careered against a hedge for 50 yards with me desperately trying to pull it back onto the right path before coming to a standstill in the middle of the road. My first reaction was to try to put it into drive as it was automatic, but it wouldn't. For the life of me, I couldn't work out why. I went out to have a look and found the back axle had snapped straight off and all the wheels caved in. Altogether it was badly damaged. I put the hazard lights on, as my car was a hazard for anyone coming over the bridge. I was stranded in the middle of nowhere, potentially in big trouble but lucky to be alive. Almost immediately, I saw a vehicle coming over the hill, so I stood in the road and flagged it down. Fortunately, it stopped without colliding with the BMW. There were two lads in the car and I offered them money to take me home. Luckily, they agreed. When I got home, I couldn't find any cash so gave them a cheque for £100. I was just thankful I got home but badly worse for wear. I went straight to bed to sleep, not thinking of the serious implications that were bound to follow. In the morning, police knocked at the door. I urged Debbie to answer it and tell them I wasn't in. Instead she stitched me up and I had no choice but to speak with them. They said my car had been left abandoned in a very dangerous place and I needed to get it moved straightaway. The copper clearly knew who I was and I'm pretty sure he realised I'd been drinking. But he basically let me off as long as I sorted out the vehicle. Gratefully, I got Graham Hodges to move it although I found out it had already been broken into and a few items stolen including my golf clubs. The cost to repair the car was £20k – notably to provide four new Alpina alloy wheels - so you can guess how bad it was.

That should have been the alarm bell to prevent me from risking it again. But, no, I was out of control. Around closing time, a guy came into the pub celebrating his birthday. Nash Baines loved a drop of the old champers and we spent another hour drinking three bottles, plus whatever else was on offer. It was then I had a moment of madness. I've had a few on the pitch in my time, as I've already told you, but this was much worse. I was one of the last customers in there and, for some reason, decided to find my keys from behind the bar. I had reached Houghton-on-the-Hill when I saw the blue lights. Immediately I knew it was a police car behind me and I was in big trouble. When I pulled up, the police officer came to the passenger side and asked me to step out of the car. Straightaway I gave the game away by attempting to climb over and out of the passenger side rather than opening my door and getting out that side. I was pissed, well pissed and wasn't thinking right. The officer asked if I'd been drinking and I told him 'yes' because it was obvious. He breathalysed me and the reading was 93 – way over the legal limit and, even worse, just over the mark that usually gets a custodial sentence. He told me to go with him to Hamilton Police Station and those 20 minutes or so was crucial as the reading came down to 89, virtually ruling out me going to prison.

Someone set me up that night. I know it. Someone phoned the police and said there was a drunk driver making his way home from The Cradock Arms. Fair play to whoever it was. No doubt about it, I hold my hands up now and realise I deserved it and the mayhem I could have caused.

I didn't stay in the cells overnight but was given a lift back home in the early hours of the morning. My aim was to keep as tightlipped as possible. I knew I was coming towards the end of my playing career and didn't want to force City's hands to let me go. I didn't tell the club straightaway although I knew it was inevitable they would find out. The person I most wanted to keep my secret from, however, was Mum. She hated anything to do with drink driving and I'd let her down very badly. She would have killed me. Being a well-known local footballer, the court case was a field day for the press. It made a front page spread on the Leicester Mercury and the local TV news as well. I was handed a two-year driving ban and fined £1,000 instead of community service. I hold my hands up I should have been locked up for a long time as I could easily have killed someone in that state.

On the pitch, with and without me, we were on yet another great League Cup run. It kicked off with a thriller against Palace as we followed up a 3-3 draw at Selhurst Park with a 4-2 victory at Filbert Street, where we also got some revenge on Grimsby by knocking them out 2-0. Next round was a real struggle against Leeds United at Filbert Street. The game finished 0-0 before we triumphed on penalties. O'Neill didn't want to risk me taking one after my miss against Tottenham and I was left admiring the coolness of several colleagues including Arnar Gunnlaugsson, the man we called the iceman; not just because he came from Iceland but because he was so super cool when it mattered most from the spot.

It was the quarter final, however, against Fulham when I started wondering whether my great run with City was coming to an end. Fulham outplayed us for long periods of the tie at Filbert Street. Paul Peschisolido put the Cottagers in front and, although I was having a particularly good game, disaster struck for me in the second half when my short pass intended for Taggart was intercepted by Peschisolido for Horsfield to make it 2-0. I remember going down on one knee in despair, dark thoughts flashing through my mind: 'It's all over, I'm finished. ' The reason I passed the ball inside to Gerry was that I was suffering from a torn groin which was killing me after kicking so many long balls. My thoughts began to clear: 'No way is this going to be the end' I said to myself. Almost immediately, I knocked the ball down for Marshy to get a goal back. There really was 'Something Inside So Strong' in Walshy right then as I ignored the groin injury to smash a powerful angled volley into the Fulham net for a late equaliser. Diving into the Kop to celebrate was a fantastic moment. It was hugely emotional for me to retrieve the situation and see the look on the fans' faces.

We knew we were going to win after that. Fulham took us all the way by holding on for a 3-3 draw after extra time before we again showed just how good we were at penalties, triumphing 3-0. I should have been over the moon afterwards – and in a way I was. After all, we were only one round away from another return trip to Wembley. But this was the point when problems in my personal life were beginning to affect my confidence and the usually super positive way I looked at things. I was a big softie underneath and quite an emotional guy. I remember being dropped off home after one game we lost, but refusing to get out at the door. Instead I walked half a mile back in pitch black and pelting rain crying - that's how much winning and losing meant to me. Being banned from driving and having worries in my family life and over how long I could stay fit enough to play the sport I loved were making me feel insecure for almost the first time in my life. The Fulham game was a landmark in how my life developed and spiralled downhill after I was kicked out of Filbert Street.

In the short term, there was plenty to look forward to as my mate Matt Elliott took his turn as a defender-turned-striker to head the only goal of our two legged semi final clash with Midland rivals Aston Villa. It was yet another famous victory for City setting up a third Wembley cup final inside four years. I would probably have been captain for a final Wembley appearance and what a way that would have been to go out. But a shocking afternoon at Chelsea changed all that. I often talk about my record of red cards with pride but there were occasions when I was left kicking myself for the damage my lack of discipline did both to me and the team.

The sending off at Stamford Bridge was perhaps the worst of the lot. The game was live on Sky TV shortly before Wembley and this cost me my place in the Worthington Cup final. I remembered an incident in a match against Blackburn Rovers when Chris Sutton stitched up Matty with a really bad eye injury. The flashpoint came when Sutty provoked me further by nipping me from behind at a free kick. Without thinking, I swung my elbow and caught him. Yet again it was the red mist, a moment of madness, and I can't defend myself in any way. Martin told me the news after the game that I was suspended from the final – and apologised. For the first time he had not warned any of the players about the danger of being ruled out. He was talking as if it was his own fault but, at the end of the day, it was stupidly mine. Altogether it cost me £40k in missed bonuses, a fine of two weeks wages but, more importantly of all, the chance to take part in another Leicester Wembley triumph.

Walshy on red cards: "Yes, I am proud of being the joint British record holder along with Roy McDonough for 13 sendings off in the Football League. Was I unlucky to get so many? No way, I should have had plenty more!

"It was remarkable Bully and I only got dismissed once each from all our clashes together. Three all was more like it. I should have gone when I head-butted Bully at Filbo and his teeth cut my head open. I used my elbow to sort out Dion Dublin against Cambridge in the play-offs and my nut on Atletico Madrid's Kiko in Europe – not to mention my antics in the tunnel on several occasions. At times, I was downright nasty.

"The only one of the 13 I would dispute was at Boro. They'd just brought in the rule about the last man and it was a nothing challenge in my book.

"Of course, I have regrets. My bad discipline cost me a shed load of money in fines and lost wages and missing out on the Wembley final against Tranmere Rovers was a killer. But, most of all, I regret costing us valuable points. Overall, it was about me and the fans. Getting hurt gave me an adrenalin rush and I did what they loved me to do and made sure I won the battle. If we were losing, we went down fighting together. Hurt them, yes; set out to injure them, no. Believe me, players know when someone has set out to get them and that would bring down my famous red mist.

"All records are there to be broken and mine will fall too – probably to a player who doesn't even get his shirt dirty. That's how much the game has changed."

I'm struggling to put into words the full story of our 'break' in La Manga that then threatened to unhinge our season. It's time to hold our hands up – we let the boss down big time on that ill-fated trip. Yet I'd argue this was an accident always waiting to happen. At Leicester City Football Club, we didn't do anything by halves – we went out onto that pitch as if our very lives depended on it and our socialising was never less than Champions League quality either. Usually, we knew the boundaries and never let the good times get in the way of the job we had to do. In fact, arguably, they helped us maintain the fantastic team spirit the whole country associated with us.

O'Neill's thinking behind sending us away for a week at a crucial stage of the season was sound enough. Cloughie did it effectively at Forest to rest aching limbs and minds and ensure the lads were fresh for the challenges ahead. O'Neill used the same tactic well – whilst others were struggling along in the British winter, we got ourselves some much-needed sun and were all the better for it. Problem was we all knew the score by now. It may have been billed as a training camp but what we were actually looking forward to was a week on the piss. Little did anyone realise we'd pack a whole week's drinking into one night!

The mistake the gaffer made – and I really don't know whether he could have altered his plans – was not coming on the trip himself. Instead he left us in the social hands of his assistant John Robertson, which only increased our idea that this was going to be one hell of a trip. To be fair, Robbo was a great bloke who I knew from my days at Wigan and worked extremely well with Martin. They were good friends and colleagues from Forest. I met former Leicester legend Peter Shilton during this year's World Cup and he rated Robbo by far the best player he ever played with. We all loved Robbo because he was a real character on top of having been a fantastic footballer. He chatted with Sheila and finished off The Sun crossword over about 20 cigarettes in the laundry room, cracked a few jokes to help us relax and could still do a turn on the training ground. Even wearing a knee brace, you could see what a talent he was every Friday in the Young v Old match. It was very difficult to take the ball off him. He was never likely to wear the yellow jersey reserved for donkey of the day. Needless to say that usually belonged to Steve Claridge! Robbo's fingers were brown due to his excessive cigarette smoking and he was a Premier League drinker, which only served to increase his popularity with the lads. He was also an enthusiastic part of our card games in which he suffered his fair share of losses. This was a part of the City set up Martin wasn't always aware of. We'd start a game on a Friday night on the bus travelling to an away game and it wasn't out of the ordinary to win or lose about £2,000.

But putting Robbo in charge of the trip was a fatal mistake. We knew he was almost certainly going to be the life and soul of the party rather than a party pooper and so it proved. The scene was set with the short flight itself. He was so scared of flying he used to cling hold of the seat in front and I swear he was white with fear even after half a dozen brandys. When we landed in Spain, he didn't walk off the plane, he fell off it - along with a few players. I made a quiet start by having a game of golf with a couple of the lads, including Phil Gilchrist and Graeme Fenton, whilst most of the others settled in at the hotel. By the time I walked in a few hours later, they were settled in alright – mostly at the bar. One of the first to join me for a meal was new signing Stan Collymore. He had only been at the club for a few weeks and we were getting on quite well. Marshy had already dumped him in it on Stan's very first away trip with us when he invited Stan to sit next to him on the team bus, knowing all too well that was my place I had for 13 years. When I walked on and told him "that's my seat, Stanley," it was a potential flashpoint. But he handled it well, quickly giving up his seat to the 'senior' player. That told me all I needed to know. Stan may have been a big shot at Liverpool and Aston Villa but, having gone through the mill in his football and private lives in more recent times, he was prepared to knuckle down and be one of the lads.

Stan was in his element in La Manga. After the meal, a group of us, including Stan, Tim Flowers, Gilly and a few young lads, went for a drink down the road to Mulligans 19th hole bar and he got the party started by ordering whisky shots to liven things up. Then he took an interest in a bottle of Jack Daniels. Not being put off by the barman's advice that he could get the same drink much cheaper over the road, he bought it and poured out our drinks before settling the 400 euro bill. As you can imagine, we carried a few of the young lads back to bed. I was on the way to having a good time myself but even I was shocked when I walked back into the hotel bar – I can only describe it as carnage. Unknown to us, former Leicester legend Gary Lineker was staying there too and he was far from happy. "This lot, Walshy, are a disgrace," he said. It was difficult to argue. I'm not sure Pontus Kaamark, our former player who was also there with Swedish friends, would have disagreed either even if he wouldn't have been surprised.

Already the hotel manager was very upset with us. There were a number of more sober guests staying there and the sight of a team of alcohol-fuelled footballers in full swing was never going to impress them. The manager went straight to Robbo as head of the party to say he was going to have to move us all into another room. Puffing away on his cigarette, drinking heavily and generally having a rip roaring time, Robbo reminded me of Oliver Reed at that moment. And Oliver Reed never stopped parties. "You're going to have to sort them out, Walshy," he told me. I did what I could to calm the problem down. I apologised to the hotel manager, accepted his decision and assured him we would be quiet from then on. Well, two out of three wasn't bad! I sat with Robbo where four of the lads were playing cards. It was around 11.30pm and Marshy asked Robbo for an extension on our midnight curfew the gaffer had set. Robbo refused but Marshy asked him to ring Martin and, at least, ask. Robbo replied "you fuckin' ring him" and threw his phone across the table. Marshy dialled Martin's number but it went straight to voicemail. Marshy said: "Hiya, gaffer, we're having a great time out here; can we stay out longer? Love you Marshy!" *Mistake number 1 – never declare your drunken undying love to the boss!*

We got louder and louder. Moved into a lounge area, where a few guests were more used to a quiet drink and someone playing on the piano, we decided to have a full scale karaoke with Lenny in full throttle and plenty of dancing. This is where I came in for some unfair criticism.

There were reports of me dancing with my trousers around my ankles and wearing red women's underwear. Admittedly, I'd had a few by this stage and couldn't remember everything that went on but the truth was I had red lining to my trousers and was definitely not exposing my feminine side! Although, on the other hand, who knows? *Mistake number 2 the karaoke, not the underwear!*

They say everything comes in threes and Stan provided the party piece. He was sitting next to me when, completely out of the blue, he picked up a fire extinguisher and let it off in the direction of physio Mick Yeoman filling the room with white powder.

That really was the last straw for the remaining guests, one of whom tried to smack Lenny. Again, I was called in as peacemaker to try to ensure an already very bad situation didn't get even worse. I got Lenny out of the firing line and ushered the guest out of the door and potential harm's way. The only thing left was to get Stan to bed and plead damage limitation. *Mistake number 3 another fine mess you got us into, Stanley.*

Plan A was to sweat off the night's alcohol with training the next morning and my alarm was set. But when I walked downstairs ready, boots in hand, Robbo was sat with some of the lads looking gloomy. "We're not training, Walshy," he said. "Brilliant, what are we doing, Robbo?" I asked, as it's always horrible training with a bad head. "We're going home!" he replied. We had been kicked out of the hotel not even 24 hours into a week's trip because of Fireman Stan!

We were in a much more sober mood on the flight home to Gatwick and knew we were in real trouble when greeted on the runway by the team bus. Marshy had been recalling his 'love you' message to the gaffer and knew he'd be in for it. We were meant to be going back to the training ground but a massive press alert meant big issues so we diverted back to Sketchley Grange for inquest time. The media still got a good shot of what appeared to be Gerry Taggart putting two fingers up as the bus drove off the runway. Infact it was my mate Muzzy having a laugh - it just looked like it was big Gerry.

There was no joking, however, when we arrived. There we were in this large conference room, still hung over from the night before and knowing we were in for the mother of all bollockings. Martin piled on the agony. He kept us waiting in that tense atmosphere for about an hour and a half before marching in from the back of the room. He was furious. And I mean furious. We'd had dressing downs before but nothing like this. He ripped off his jacket and tore into us. Fingers were mainly pointed in three directions – Marshy, Stan and myself. Marshy was first and left in no doubt that, should he ever phone the gaffer again late at night, he'd be signing his own death warrant at Leicester City; Stan was singled out as being the head of the party and for his fire extinguisher stunt; and I took a hit because, as captain, I should have kept everyone in order.

All three got fined two weeks wages and, in my case, I still think that was harsh. Responsibility had been handed over to me by Robbo and I'd done my best to keep a lid on things. But, honestly, it was impossible. Had the story on the dance floor been true, I'd have taken my punishment on the chin. But it wasn't. Overall, I was fairly proud of the way I acted but that was one time being skipper and senior player counted against me. Another consolation was that I missed La Manga two!

Being suspended for the cup final was a huge blow. We were so proud of our League Cup achievements and I'd have given anything to be out there as we aimed to bring home the trophy. I had helped us all the way there and deserved to be playing at Wembley for what would have been my eighth time. In addition, after losing two weeks wages for the red card at Chelsea and another two for La Manga, my wages that month were £0.00!

O'Neill was good to the players who weren't available for the final against First Division Tranmere Rovers inviting new signing Collymore, who wasn't eligible for the cup tie, the injured Darren Eadie and me to stay with the rest of the squad in London. He wanted to keep our group spirit and was usually happy for the ones who were injured or suspended to get as pissed as they liked. We never needed telling twice! We stayed at a top class hotel overnight in London where, for obvious reasons, the three of us who knew we weren't playing were keen to go out for the night. Stan was desperate. He virtually begged the boss to allow us out. The last thing O'Neill wanted after La Manga was any more unrest but Stan said he had a driver who would look after all of us and ensure we were back by a reasonable time. Gaffer said no three times but gave in finally and said our deadline was midnight. Happy days for us and off we went!

We started out at a club called the Atlantic Rooms where we met up with a big City fan called Andy Bottrill, from Admiral Cleaning, a good friend of mine and a box holder at Filbert Street. He was very pleased to see us and quickly ordered champagne for our table which got the night off to a bubbly start. When we decided to move on he came with us. At our next venue, he took part in a game called Spoof. It was a guessing game with a maximum of three coins. All you had to do was guess the total that everyone was holding. Anyway Stan started to get big time and raised the stakes to three grand a man. My arse fell out straightaway; I'm not Steve Claridge and don't give a shit but couldn't pull out when everyone else had agreed. Eadie was first to get safe, then me - what a relief as the loser was going to pay everyone £3K. The night got a lot worse for Stan as Andy then guessed right. So Stan signed an 'I owe you' to Andy for £12k but Andy couldn't find his wallet. He wasn't pulling a fast one because it had genuinely been stolen – cash, cards and match tickets all included. I had my suspicions who had taken it but will leave it at that. Let's just say not all of Stan's friends had a heart of gold. I never remember Stan actually paying and think Andy still has the slip.

At least, Stan's driver was on the money as he got us back to the hotel by midnight – just a few minutes before curfew time. Then Stan had a bright idea. The gaffer had only said we needed to be back in the hotel by midnight, nothing about having to be in bed. The better option, by far, was to seek out the hotel bar. Stan and I were enthusiastically greeted by a family from Liverpool, who were staying in the same hotel and immediately recognised Stan. There was a grandfather in a wheelchair, a father and two daughters. We joined them and were soon enjoying a chat and a drink. The atmosphere got a bit more tense for Stan when one of the daughters started asking him about his affair with Ulrika Jonsson. He refused to talk about it but it made me laugh because the lads had asked him the same question when he first arrived at the club and he laughed it off saying the Swede had a 'fat arse and saggy tits'.

Suddenly Stan told me he was going to the toilet and could I look after his leather jacket? I'd been drinking for a fair while by this point and it took me a while to realise he'd been gone too long. Problems started when the same thing clicked with the girl's father. He jumped up and screamed "my fuckin' daughter!" I got up to chase him but was tripped by the grandad in the wheelchair and fell over before staggering on through reception area to find out what was happening. The guy had Stan by the throat threatening him. Not for the first time in my life, I found myself in the very difficult situation of 'peacemaker'. I managed to separate the father from Stan and then he threatened me saying "I want you outside!" "Come on, then," I replied. All of a sudden, two policemen rushed into reception so I ushered Stan up into the lift and out of harm's way with the family now having left the hotel. I told Stan "stay in my room. don't wake Heskey up" and all Stan kept saying to me was "Walshy, please don't say anything, this is bad!" I told him to shut up and get some sleep. But, if we thought that was the end of the matter, we were wrong. O'Neill was in my hotel at 8am, his glasses in my face, saying we were both a "fucking disgrace" and to get out of the hotel immediately. He wanted us as far away from the match day party as possible so we were kicked out of the hotel. We had to pay to have a few hours of sleep in the Sanderson Hotel, a favourite of Stan's, and persuade secretary Andy Neville to give us a couple of match tickets. In short, we watched the game at Wembley in disgrace. Naturally I was thrilled by Matty's two goals and our 2-1 victory that brought the cup back to Leicester yet again but the previous night certainly took the edge off my celebrations.

That was one occasion when I don't think I did an awful lot wrong although I'm not one to bash Stan. Far from it. I got on very well with him and think that, on the whole, he did his best to knuckle down to life under O'Neill. He gave me the impression that he knew the score without having to be told. He had a reputation as a hell-raiser from his days at Forest, Liverpool and Villa but realised he was going to have to fit in with us. We were a tight knit dressing room who'd been through a lot together and were very united with no real superstars throwing their weight around. Stan had a lot of respect for what we'd achieved and knew he wouldn't be top dog with us. For O'Neill, handling a guy who'd caused a lot of problems elsewhere was a challenge he was well up for. Like Cloughie in the past, he backed himself to get the best out of a very talented player and make light of the baggage he brought with him. City fans who saw Stan's hat trick in a 5-2 victory over Sunderland will probably agree with me when I say he could have been with us a lot longer and played a bigger part in our future but for Tater Peeler. As with Tony Cottee and me, the new manager took one look at Stan and wanted him out. He couldn't cope with bigger people and personalities being at the same football club. He and Leicester City were the losers….

O'Neill was good enough to hand me a new one-year deal and say he'd always consider me to be part of the furniture at Leicester City. I didn't see his departure coming, to be honest, because I wasn't too concerned about what was going on behind the scenes. We were in a very healthy position, both as a team and a club. We'd just finished eighth in probably the best league in the world and won a cup. Also, the bank balance was more than healthy, particularly as we'd just pocketed a cool £11m from the sale of big Emile to Liverpool. Perhaps he wanted to leave us at the top. Perhaps the lure of Celtic, a massive football club, was too much for him to refuse. But the day he walked out the door, my fate was effectively sealed, let's be honest. I felt he gave me the contract as a token of good will for everything I had done for him.

Walshy on Martin O'Neill: "Martin was always his own man. It was said that he and his manager Brian Clough had a love-hate relationship at Forest yet he liked Old Big Head enough to invite him down the Leicester City training ground quite often.

"My relationship with O'Neill was probably love-hate too. We got on famously most of the time, but had plenty of fall outs mostly due to my unpredictable life. He didn't like clever remarks and could jump on anyone, me included, like a ton of bricks. You knew who was in charge, put it that way. But he'd never be down on me for long. He always allowed me a way back into his good books and, if I saw him today, we'd be the best of friends.

"Martin was a great manager; the best I ever worked with. During his half time talk, he'd always protect anyone who was having an off day. He often blasted us but in a way that would motivate us to force a result. I didn't always remember a single word he said, but got the message. As with Cloughie, Martin's art was we never knew what to expect. That famous day at Derby when we were 4-0 up after 20-odd minutes, we came in at half time expecting to be praised – instead we got a real pasting to ensure we didn't dare take it easy – a great example of his man management.

"He also had that knack of knowing players he could have a real go at and those who needed an arm around the shoulder. It was no secret, however, that Steve Guppy was his blue-eyed boy, alongside Muzzy, who also could do little wrong. One guy who took him to the brink and beyond was Lenny and, I suppose, Claridge came into that bracket. They were able to get away with things that others couldn't and wound up O'Neill big time on many occasions. Unlike McGhee, O'Neill was much happier to see me smash the ball into Row Z rather than take the slightest chance of being caught in possession. That was great by me because I was brought up never to take chances in defensive areas.

"Martin was a very passionate guy who rarely forgot anything. As widely reported, he received one letter from an unhappy Leicester fan claiming he wasn't good enough for the post when things weren't going well in those early days – and kept it. Then on the night we were celebrating promotion to the Premier League after beating Crystal Palace, he phoned the letter writer at 11pm and gave him a piece of his mind. I got much the same treatment when I came into his office to have a word – he'd remember all I'd done wrong in the past and I never stood a chance of winning any argument.

"He was fascinated by crime and the legal world. He was particularly keen on finding out anything he could about the Yorkshire Ripper and when in Tampa took time out to visit the empty cell once occupied by Lee Harvey Oswald, the sniper who killed US President John F Kennedy.

"When manager of Celtic, Martin invited me, Gupps, and Muzzy to a home game and treated us like kings. He made sure we were very well looked after and, after Celtic had won the match 1-0, had some beers with us taking time to ask how we were all getting on. He took me into the home dressing room at Parkhead sat me down and asked about my personal problems.

"I had no doubt Martin genuinely cared whether I was alright which I really appreciated.

"It's great to see him back in management again after all his own family worries. I loved seeing him as a pundit during the World Cup – and was delighted he gave Leicester a mention. All the best, Martin!"

I honestly thought I could become Leicester City's new manager, working with Tony Cottee. Some folk would take a look at my lifestyle and scoff at such a view. But I knew what I had to give and that was 100 per cent commitment to the club and the fact we would have both been totally accepted by that dressing room. Who knows what could have been? The odds were stacked against us because of our lack of managerial experience and our lack of qualifications, which we were both more than willing to put right.

We made our pitch on the idea we could keep the dressing room together, even more vital after such a successful manager had just gone. But even the circumstances of our meeting with board members, including chairman Martin George, told the story. It was at Luton Airport, with George about to go on holiday, which hinted to us he was going through the motions. Nevertheless I think they were impressed with our professional presentation and several new signings we could put in the frame including striker Chris Sutton. Yes, I had my personal run-ins with him but he was a quality player and a physical force who could have done us a great job.

I would have knuckled down under Taylor. I knew no other way and my heart was still with Leicester City. Taylor himself praised the way I worked that pre-season and could see I was injury free and ready for the new campaign. But he was never honest or up front with me. I played in all the pre-season tour games in Holland as Gerry Taggart was injured and he gave me the very strong impression I'd done well enough to be first choice in that match against West Ham United early in the Premier League campaign. As late as the Monday before the game, he reassured me this was still the case but come the trip to Upton Park Taggart was restored to the starting line up and I was only on the bench. I came on as substitute and got one last memento to mark what turned out to be my final ever appearance for City – the shirt of future England skipper Rio Ferdinand, who shortly afterwards broke the British transfer record with his £18m move to Leeds United.

Things were not looking good for me, either on the training ground or on the pitch. To be honest, I found Taylor's methods too basic. More like a schoolteacher than a football manager in his manner, all he could come up with were five yard training drills, better suited to teenagers than top professionals who'd been there and won medals. Mind you, even they were often too demanding for our new signing Ade Akinbiyi – and I'm not kidding. I don't want to have a go at a great guy who ran his heart out for Leicester City but his £5m transfer from Wolves highlighted everything that started to go wrong. Talent-wise he wasn't in the same league as Hesk, yet he wasn't the worst of Taylor's signings – midfielder Junior Lewis, in particular, would have struggled to get a game with many lower division sides.

When Taylor's staff weren't telling me about the next club who were supposedly interested in me, he was threatening to run me up and down the stands. I knew he was trying to punish me to push me out the door – something I recognised from previous managers with other players.

Some folk may think my view of Peter Taylor was sour grapes. But later events proved he was the wrong man for Leicester City. He took over a very good side with plenty of cash in the bank and managed to squander all of it and send the club into crisis. In all, he reportedly spent £26m and bought very badly. What the fans may not know is that he also increased the wages of moderate players very dramatically.

Truth was Taylor wasn't comfortable with big personalities at the football club because he wasn't a big personality himself. That's why he kicked Collymore, Cottee and I into touch as fast as possible. Ok, no harm in putting an emphasis on youth but his team needed balance and experience, for me, in such a demanding league. Instead he let it slip through his fingers when we could all have added another season's value to our squad.

The penny finally dropped when Taylor announced his 18-man squad for the UEFA Cup tie against Red Star Belgrade – and I wasn't in it. If I couldn't even make the 18 for such an important game, I had no future under this manager. Had Taylor been a man, he would have chatted things through with me properly. Had he argued my better days were behind me because of all the injuries, I would have accepted it. I would have known I was valued and respected but time had caught up with me. But he did none of that. Instead he passed the buck to others to tell me about other clubs being interested and tried to make my life as miserable as possible.

As I wrote earlier, my mind was a complete mess. Even Nottingham Forest was suggested as a club that might be interested in taking me on. How on earth could I play for them after all those years with the Blue Army? When I went to Wolves and saw a young Julian Lescott, later to play for England, looking impressive in training, it was yet another twist of the knife. Here was a young guy at the beginning of his career with everything to look forward to; very suddenly, I felt I was at the end.

Steve Walsh's feats have entered into Club folk lore and they resulted in him topping the Leicester City voting in the 2004 BBC TV 'Football Focus' poll to find out who the fans regarded as their all-time cult hero. This was no surprise. For fans he embodied total passion and commitment to the cause. Although this resulted in far too many red cards, his never-say-die attitude throughout his career will always be remembered and admired by Leicester's supporters. His legendary clashes with Steve Bull live in the memory!

The record books show that during his 14 years at the club, many as skipper, he made 449 appearances, scored 62 goals and appeared in six out of the seven Wembley appearances Leicester made between 1992 and 2000. He missed the seventh through suspension. These statistics don't begin to capture the essence of Steve's contribution to Leicester's cause over the years.

He seems to have been central to many of the most memorable moments in the club's recent history.

One of the most famous photographs in the club's history is of Steve celebrating immediately after scoring the second, winning goal against Derby County. I nearly broke my hand when Steve scored. I was up in the Olympic Gallery at Wembley. When Steve scored, I jumped up, raising my fist in the air. It crashed into the steel roof of the Olympic Gallery which was lower than I realised. It was a painful drive back to Leicester. Steve's shirt, boots and medal from this great occasion are now on display in Reception at King Power Stadium, along with all of his other Leicester City medals.

John Hutchinson, Leicester City historian and archivist

Chapter Eight

Hitting Rock Bottom

My biggest regret is that I should have
handled things better for the sake of the children

NOTHING hit home harder. I sat around the breakfast table telling my children
I was leaving. In my heart of hearts, I knew for months, even years, this moment
was coming – although that didn't make it any easier. The bewildered looks on
my children's faces showed it was a shock to them. They were never likely to
see the situation from my point of view. It would be a long time before they'd
forgive me - if ever – whatever I said. I hadn't been happy for years but, thanks to
football, that pain had been buried until I could deny it no more. What I daren't
admit, either to them or to myself, was that it wasn't just my marriage to Debbie
that was in ruins – it was my whole life.

As far as the break up was concerned, I could have no complaints. Football
and women had gone hand in hand. I lived by the rock star life, now I died by
it. But that wasn't all. I wasn't particularly happy at home and that affected my
behaviour. Most of my conquests were one-offs, but deep down I was actually
looking for the perfect woman and to settle down. Now I realise searching for
happiness is part of being human, isn't it? This book is the truth of my life but
there are at least a couple of areas where I'm not prepared to go. One of them
was a deep problem in my relationship with Debbie that I only found out about
shortly after we got married and was always likely to cause us problems. For a
long, long time I tried to ignore it, helped by the fact that my focus was on my
football and that makes you quite single minded and selfish.

At the height of my womanising it got so bad I climbed out of beds in the
morning scarcely knowing where I was or who I'd been with. How on earth

Debbie didn't find out earlier, I honestly will never know. There were so many narrow escapes it was unbelievable really. One good example was when we were living in Burton-on-the-Wolds and I was knocking off a woman from the next village. I took her to a playing field in my car and things began to get hot. Only problem was that the baby seat in the back was getting in the way. So one thing had to go. I threw the baby seat out onto the field and carried on regardless. I'd forgotten about the potential problem the next day when Debbie went into the car and asked where the baby seat was. That was a difficult question, so I told her I hadn't got a clue and played for time. Later that day, I rushed back to the field and, thankfully, the baby seat was still there and intact. So I put it back into the car and told my wife I'd just remembered I'd put it in the boot. Luckily, I got away with that one. Let's face it, it was probably a more likely story from someone so absent minded than the actual truth!

My luck finally ran out when I was on a golfing holiday with Alan Clancy, who used to look after the team on our pre season adventures in Ireland and subsequently became a good friend. Many a weekend I'd play a Premier League game, get on a flight from East Mids to Dublin and be watching the highlights on Sky TV with a few beers within a couple of hours or so of the final whistle.

I went away with him to unwind after some stressful games and things were going well until a phone call from Debbie. "You've been having an affair, Steve," she said. My instinct was to immediately deny it but I had nowhere to hide as the woman I'd been going out with for a year on and off - now off – was sitting next to Debbie as she was making the call. Denise was a pretty blonde who, unlike a lot of my women, turned out to be more serious about me. Most were more than happy just to have fun and the fact I was married was probably an advantage rather than a problem. They knew what they wanted and so did I. But Denise was playing for keeps. Worrying words she had said came back into my mind: "If you ever break up with me, I'll haunt you." Those words scared me and she lived up to her threat. I ended the call and left the two women to fight over my future. My golf went downhill from that point!

It was the biggest decision of my life to move out of my family home, leave my three children and live in the Holiday Inn. Words can't describe how I felt seeing their little faces watching me go. It still haunts me to this day. I had to do it for myself really. I had a choice to make: do I live unhappily for the rest of my life or do I leave? Dad's principles were to stay and see it through however unhappy I was but Mum's were very different – she understood me more than anyone. I decided I had to go.

I'd be naïve if I said being kicked out of Leicester City caused all my problems. It didn't. It just brought them all to the surface. The cracks had been there for everyone to see – apart from me. Infidelities, drinking and wild living, coupled with stretching my body beyond reasonable limits, all took their toll. Depression, yes, depression – had begun to take its invisible hold. How could it happen to Steve Walsh? I was the guy, let's remember, who ran through walls. On the pitch, no challenge was too big. I was Captain Fantastic, the toast of the Blue Army, and fearless to the point of extreme recklessness. But I realise now that I'd been falling headlong into a dark hole for at least a year before I left Leicester. Fearful thoughts which flooded my mind following that weird injury against Arsenal had terrible consequences. Yes, I'd been 'guilty' of drinking and driving many times before and I'm not proud of it. But it was an act of complete madness to pick up those car keys in the Cradock Arms. What could I have been thinking? I believe now I was suffering from a cocktail of stress, shock and depression, as well as alcohol excess. Together all these problems certainly hit me head on, like a high speed train.

Had I not been depressed, joining Norwich City could have been a joy rather than something I dreaded. A very friendly and good football club was prepared to pick me off the scrapheap and give me a future. I was handed a two-year contract on £5,000 a week, more than I'd been paid throughout my entire career with Leicester, plus the chance to make a new start in Norfolk. In addition, I was given personal lifelines to hang onto from my past – I was joining up for a third time with manager Bryan Hamilton, a good man who had faith in me, and playing in the same team as former City colleagues Tony Cottee and Iwan Roberts. In normal circumstances, I should have felt at home.

But there was denial on both sides. True, I got myself physically fit after a few weeks in Norfolk but no way could I have passed a rigorous medical. Instead they put me through a few very routine tests because, they desperately wanted me on board. On my part, I wasn't honest with Norwich. I told them I was raring to go and ready for the challenge when my tortured mind was saying the total opposite. Inside I was collapsing even faster than my body was failing – and that's saying something!

Travelling to Norwich daily on the train from Oakham wasn't ideal. It was during these traumatic months that problems in my marriage were hitting home. Add everything up and I was never in a position to give Norwich the service they deserved. Some days I stayed at The Post House Hotel in Norwich but mostly I was commuting. When I arrived at the club, I walked into the usual Bryan Hamilton crisis meetings I'd sat through so many times at both Wigan and Leicester. I'd be there for two hours whilst the manager was tackling the team's struggles in the First Division. Instead of thinking about what he was saying, I was wondering what on earth I was doing there. I just couldn't wait to catch the train back.

I'd be dropped off at Oakham for the daily two-hour journey to Norwich. I was supposed to be ready to train by 10am but that was always a struggle. I'd arrive at the railway station at about 9.35am, then be in the expert hands of Joe, the taxi driver, who raced me across the city at the speed of light to get to the training ground on time. To his credit, he almost always got me there at about bang on 10am although, by then, I should have been changed and ready. Usually, I'd be chasing around at the end of my day for the train back home. Thanks again to Joe, still a good mate to this day, I usually made it. But the very stressful schedule didn't help me at all.

One nice thing that happened was a friendship with a fellow train passenger. A blind man was very often making the same journey from Oakham to Norwich. Not particularly interested in football, he was a nice guy I'd sometimes help onto the train with his Labrador. Debbie was dropping me at the station one day as I was due to play in a reserve match on a Wednesday night at Norwich when I spotted him about half a mile away in the rain. I knew where he was heading, so asked her to leave me there so I could walk with him to the station. It was pissing it down and I felt a bit sorry for him, so much so I lost my concentration. We'd been on the train for quite a while when I saw signs for Sheffield and Doncaster. We were going in completely the wrong direction! I asked the blind man and he explained he was going to see his relatives and not going to Norwich at all. Classic Walshy luck! No way could I get to Norwich in time. I phoned the club and explained what had happened. I don't think they believed me because it sounded like a tall story – but, this time, it was true!

I didn't play very often for Norwich and, when I did, I found it tough with my fitness not being the best. I had a particularly disastrous debut at Wolves where we got beat 4-0. It was my only start for the Canaries and I struggled to come to grips with the game before being substituted. I'd done a great deal of physical work under Bryan's very strict regime, but still wasn't properly fit. The defeat wasn't all my fault – my team mates made their fair share of mistakes - but the writing was on the wall.

I always had time for Hamilton and he was good for me both at Wigan and then signing me for Leicester. But I wasn't blind to his weaknesses either and they were on full show at Carrow Road. Bryan was a manager who got too involved with his players and fell out with a percentage of them. That left him vulnerable when results weren't going his way. This ended with more bad news for me when Hamilton was dismissed and his assistant Nigel Worthington stepped up into the hot seat. That move definitely finished me off in East Anglia. Hamilton had time for me because I'd served him well in the past, but Worthington was different. He saw me as a threat, perhaps thinking I'd fancy another crack at management after applying at Leicester. He couldn't have been more wrong on that score but had a point that I was on big wages. I was still only a third of the way through my contract and wasn't involved in the first team at all. Worthington's tactics, as Taylor's had been, were designed to break my spirit so I'd run out the door. I was training with the kids – anything to piss me off.

I was never going to be crazy enough to pack my bags but was definitely in the market for a compromise. We came to an agreement with me being paid a handsome sum, but still losing around £200,000 on my original deal. I was more than happy to sign the settlement and get out of the door. I do feel a debt to Norwich fans for my unhappy time there. I hope that when Canaries supporters read this and realise how near the edge I was physically – but even more so mentally – they will understand why they never saw the best of me at Carrow Road. I never gave less than 100 per cent on any football field yet, for the reasons I've been writing about, I just didn't have the heart any more during that bleak time in my career; my sadness was I wanted to still be at Leicester City. During the writing of this book, I spoke with Norwich fans in a radio interview and apologised further for the way I let them down. None of it was their fault. They were a fantastic club and I just wish I could have shown them the real Walshy.

Even Leicester City temporarily going to the top of the Premier Division that winter was no great consolation for me. I didn't get too excited because I honestly knew it wouldn't last. Being proved right was no fun. Taylor's team faded dramatically in the last ten games of the season to finish below mid-table and within 12 months City had been relegated and the manager was gone. He'd wasted everything that O'Neill had built and let City fans down very badly as well as destroying me.

My next football move was perhaps more realistic as I went into Non League for the first time in my career to team up with former City mate Gary Mills at Tamworth. Millsy invited me to come and have a game with his team who were aiming to get promotion into the Conference. I said yes mostly as a favour to Millsy. My most memorable day there was the last of the season at Folkestone when we had to win to achieve our aim. I scored one of our goals and won a penalty late on that would have given us victory. But, in a cruel twist of fate, the kick was missed and a frantic 3-3 draw kept us down.

Then Millsy got a job working under another former Fox Gary McAllister at Coventry City and I was very briefly back in the big time again on a game by game deal. Although there's a lot of feeling between the clubs, I thought I was on good ground playing under two former Leicester players and alongside my good mate Julian Joachim. Jules was not only a very good player when he was at Filbert Street but a lad I socialised a lot with and even went into business with. We had many a good time together at Willie Thorne's Snooker Centre, helped by the fact that Jules was a massive gambler. I still remind him every now and again of an afternoon we had playing 'Shell'. It involved potting a red, then picking up a numbered bottle top out of a bag to decide the coloured ball. If you potted the colour and it was your number after a red, then boom the money pot was yours. I won £500 from him in the first frame. By the end I was £13,500 in pocket, but never saw any of the cash. Those were great days playing snooker, pool and gambling when we had nothing else to do after training. Running a Chinese restaurant together at the bottom of New Walk was a more serious business. There's no reason why it couldn't have been a success with up to 180 people eating there but, as with everything else I touched around that time, it all went wrong. I came into the business as a third party working with Julian, Sean Taylor, the lottery winner, and a guy called Tan (no relation to the present owner of Cardiff City!). I actually put £30,000 of my own cash into that restaurant but never saw anything in return. It didn't help that the chefs were selling ducks, prawns and scallops out the back to their mates and was made a whole lot worse when Mr Tan ran off with all of my money never to be seen again.

Officials at Coventry welcomed me with open arms despite my Leicester connections but my latest on-field partnership with Julian was no more successful. I only played a couple of games for the Sky Blues, including a 5-2 away defeat at Watford and my professional career was finally dead and buried. That proved to be my last Football League appearance and was a harrowing experience. Our defence was a complete shambles and made me look worse than I actually was. Although we had experienced players, our full backs weren't on the same wavelength and constantly left us exposed. I was taken off well before the end.

Millsy didn't last long either and his return to Tamworth gave me an opportunity to play third fiddle to him and Darren Gee at The Lamb. That was a far happier time as we got promotion and reached the FA Trophy final at Villa Park where we were disappointingly beaten 2-1 by Shaun Teale's Burscough. I could have been with the club longer but for a couple of unfortunate incidents. Millsy had a few clashes with the chairman over funding for the club and I got involved when I said a few words over the microphone urging him to dip into his pocket more to back the manager in a higher league. Not surprisingly that didn't go down too well.

Much worse, however, was when I applied for the manager's job at Grantham Town. That was the only managerial job I ever went for except for Leicester City. The Lincolnshire club, who once boasted Martin O'Neill as their boss, were ambitious in those days and it was a post that definitely interested me. I went for an interview and asked them specifically not to mention my interest to Tamworth, but they dropped me right in it. So I was out on my ear at Tamworth and not offered the Grantham post either. My options were becoming narrower all the time. Where could go I go from there?

Don't ask me how but I went into local football with my final days being spent alongside manager Stu Dealey at Leicestershire Senior League side Anstey Nomads. I played a few games and was also co-manager for about a year. Stu was a real character, a great guy who liked to look after his players including buying their boots and lending them money he never got back. He was a very distinctive figure with his blonde dyed hair but certainly knew how to win a football match at that level. The way he prepared the team for a cup final at Cropston Road was something else. He told them all that we had two new strikers for this game. The lads had already done their warm up when he ordered them back into the dressing room for a rub down. There he introduced them to two strippers from Nottingham he'd hired for the occasion. These were our new strikers! Let's put it this way, they went fully at it to make sure the players were up for the match. Needless to say I'd never seen anything like it in my career before, but it worked as the team won 6-0.

Domestically my life was a rollercoaster after leaving Debbie with new relationships intermingled with a spiralling dispute with my ex and mother of my children which eventually brought me to my financial knees. Top and bottom of the matter was that a financial pot of £1m was melted down to nothing inside just a few disastrous years. The increasingly bitter war between Debbie and I, which made it difficult at times for me to see the children, led to a far worse divorce than I thought. I remember times when I had to physically break into my own house to get my stuff; things were that bad.

Obviously I do have some sympathy with Debbie, after all she had three kids to raise. Being a footballer's wife wasn't something I would have envied during those days – and probably isn't too much different today. I was selfish as a footballer, giving the sport and my career the number one place and that can't have been ideal for her. I feel that I provided well for her and the family, being able to give them materially what they wanted, but there were many times when I wasn't there for her. The divorce settlement isn't however a moral judgement on who was or wasn't to blame for the break up of the marriage and I feel that I was the big loser in that one, although Debbie probably sees it differently. From my standpoint, she took most of the money, which has helped her to bring up the family.

I was dealt another big blow by the fact that I took the full weight of a failing investment plan that has since led to bankruptcy. It was a sound enough plan putting money into property and had I kept up my investments I would have been fine. Unfortunately I was hit by lack of cash and left with a huge liability. I felt that Debbie should shoulder half of this as I took out the plan whilst we were together but that, too, was thrown out by the court. I also lost £170,000 on my pension when the stock market crashed as I'd put it into stocks and shares. Later Debbie also took me to court for private school fees. It cost me 21 grand and her 13, if I remember correctly, and she came out with £5,000! From then, she never came back for more money.

My biggest regret is that I should have handled things better for the sake of the children. But again my lifestyle didn't help. I was drinking more to escape reality and my depression was getting worse. None of this was helped by the fact that, free from the stricter routine of football, I could live how I pleased.

Another regret I certainly have is how I treated Lynette and her family. She had been good to me for several years cleaning the house and was the person who kindly got me out of the Holiday Inn and took me into her home in Barrow to try to soften the blow. It was there that I built up a really nice relationship with her daughter Brenda whom I soon moved in with. She was a great girl I would have settled with but my mind was still in turmoil. One night I went out to a hotel and bumped into Michelle, a beauty therapist I knew from my Leicester City days and fancied like mad. It was a case of instant attraction. None of it was Brenda's fault in any way but I had to tell her and Lynette that I was on my way. I shit on both of them and I'm not proud of that. It was wrong time, wrong place for Walshy. They are still my good friends and I still see them.

Chapter Nine

Home is Where the Heart is – at Last!

Returning to England in 2006 I literally had
to pick my life back up from scratch

My first proper sighting of Steve was in The Lounge Bar in Allendale Road in July 2007. I popped in for a drink as I was taking my friend Aysha, from London, to the railway station. Steve was at the bar with his friend and they continued to send some champagne in our direction.

As we left, we caught each other's eye and ended up chatting. His friend got straight to the point and asked me for my number, saying it was for Steve. Little did I realise, it was actually for himself. However after trying his luck, he knew he wasn't getting anywhere and finally decided to pass my number to Steve.

Although I knew there was a big age difference and I was warned by a number of people not to get involved, I took my chance as I saw something different in Steve and he certainly did wine and dine me like a gentleman.

When we started going out, it came as a shock to me how much alcohol was involved in his life. There were times when he'd go missing for a couple of days and I couldn't contact him and days when he struggled to get out of bed, saying he felt better staying there. That's when I knew his depression and alcohol was taking over. It was hard at times and we had a number of arguments, always about his alcohol. I could see he was struggling with depression and starting to have anxiety attacks.

I'm so glad though I was never a footballer's wife: I don't think I could have coped with that. Funnily enough, I'd been a City fan as a youngster and even went down to the Belvoir Drive training ground with a friend to get the players' autographs. My favourite player was Iwan Roberts. We called Steve the grumpy one in defence!

You might think Steve is very brave, but that's not totally true. Through my pregnancy, we tried to get ourselves prepared for the labour however I could see the panic on Steve's face when we spoke about it. My waters broke six weeks early and the labour was traumatic. I lost three litres of blood and had three transfusions. I don't remember a whole lot as I was drifting in and out of consciousness and was struggling to breathe. However I do remember five doctors running in and out of the room. Steve was just amazing though and kept me going when I needed him most. The result was Zaki, another good looking Walsh in the family!

Steve is now much more of a family man. He will now pick up the phone and invite his daughter Olivia to Sunday dinner and it's important to me that the whole family grows together including all of his children. He still feels upset about his past and it hasn't been easy for me to read some of it in this book. But he really wants to get it right this time – and I'm here to help him do that.

SIRA WALSH, Steve's wife

I CAN still make a perfectly good case why I disappeared to Spain. My life was in total chaos and the idea of a new start, particularly with Michelle, was hugely attractive.

My finances, due to the tax burden and the disastrous divorce from Debbie, were taking me down. I was sinking fast and becoming a tax exile seemed the only option left. I was going to a place I knew very well and liked a great deal. I'd enjoyed holidays in Cabopino, where Chaz Hawley, a mate from Manchester, owned a timeshare business for 20 years. I told myself that, when I finished football, I'd love to live there. It was only surprising I hadn't done it earlier. I spoke things through with my advisor Jon Morris, who has a sound financial head on, and he agreed what I was doing was in my best interest.

Michelle was a terrific girl and I thought it was meant to be when we got together. Everything seemed to be pointing in the same direction. I could put problems that were bringing me down to the back of my mind and start a new life in paradise. The following three years, however, taught me a very important life lesson: you can run a million miles, but you always take your problems with you. What I'm talking about is not the bankruptcy, divorce or alcohol abuse, but my tortured mind that was the real root of it all. Going to Spain was an escape and reality was always waiting to bite back.

The timing also seemed right because for the first and only time in my whole life I'd fallen out with football and Leicester City. After being kicked out of the door as a player, I made a mini comeback as a co-commentator with Radio Leicester. The role appealed to me as I was being paid to watch the club I cared so much for but even that backfired. I've always been honest and up front with the fans and they appreciated that. As a player, I wouldn't say we'd played well if we hadn't. My emotions were very similar to the loyal folk who paid their hard earned cash to watch us play. That's one of the major reasons why we had this remarkable bond between us that continues to this day. I wasn't going to change that for the radio. The problem was that criticising players wasn't just a matter between me and the listeners. The club didn't like it and weren't slow in letting me know. I was being put in a difficult position in which I didn't feel welcome coming to the Walkers Stadium to do my job.

It didn't help that this was probably the lowest stage in the club's history. Following hard on surviving a very serious financial meltdown, promotion and relegation, the Foxes were now in the ambitious hands of businessman Milan Mandaric. He announced a three-year plan to take us back into the Premier League but instead we were heading in the opposite direction. I had no problem with Milan – he was always fine with me and wanted City to succeed. Yet we became a comedy club for a while going through a quick succession of managers – from Rob Kelly when he took over to Nigel Worthington, Martin Allen, Gary Megson and Ian Holloway before Nigel Pearson first started to point us back in the right direction. However I will say this. Milan came here with a reputation of being a ruthless businessman and didn't disappoint. He was here for a few years and made a few bob and did us a huge, huge favour by introducing us to the current Thai owners who have proved so good for us. Milan was always good with me, sparing time to chat and being very welcoming. I've got no complaints.

Walshy on meeting former City boss Martin Allen: "I bumped into him by mistake when looking for my mate Simon Grayson. Larry was the manager of Blackpool, City's opponents on the first day of the season, and we arranged to meet at the Marriott Hotel in Leicester for a drink on the Friday night. I walked in and spotted Simon at the end of the bar. As I leant across to shake his hand, this guy in a white sweat top with drink stains tried to say hello. Instinctively I tried to excuse myself and talk to Simon, having no idea I was just ignoring the new City boss.

"It wasn't me being rude – I just didn't recognise the bloke. I didn't expect a football manager to be dressed like that. He was scruffy and very animated and I didn't know what to make of him. For some reason, he reminded me of Jim Carey, the American comedy actor. Once introduced, we chatted together happily enough but it didn't surprise me too much that Allen's stay at City was so short. I think he got on the wrong side of owner Milan Mandaric by trying to change things too quickly. Some of the rules such as nobody was allowed to walk past his office window were just silly and eccentric."

Allen was in charge and I was at the City Ground on a bleak night which put a lot of things into perspective. That was when our full back Clive Clarke, on loan from Sunderland, suffered a heart attack during the half time interval and I witnessed how close he was to not pulling through. It was touch and go for a long time in that dressing room before he was finally brought back round. Understandably, the shock scared our lads and they were in no state to come out for the second half. Forest, to their great credit, did the right thing by calling off the match, even though they were 1-0 up and playing well. When the tie was replayed and Megson was in the City hot seat, we made a great return gesture – apparently ordered by Milan – to allow Forest goalkeeper Paul Smith to walk through our defence from the opening whistle to give them their goal back, Rivals or no rivals, sportsmanship and decency won the day – even better Leicester won 3-2!

Things went from bad to worse on the pitch and the decision to bring in Ian Holloway to rescue a potentially disastrous season didn't work either. In my view he made a number of tactical errors in our fight against relegation.

The manager lost the plot with us at Radio Leicester and the rest of the press as he could see his job prospects ebbing away as results went against us. One memorable example was after an away game at Cardiff when Holloway lost his temper totally with commentator Jon Barber during a recorded interview. Jon told me when he got back to the car, physically shaking, that Holloway had made a huge gaffe during their after match chat and ordered it be edited out as he knew he'd be in hot water. Jon refused and he claimed the angry manager had physically threatened him. During the journey home, Jon was on the phone speaking to his bosses about what to do. It was so serious the radio station decided not to broadcast it.

I was also at the microphone that fateful Sunday afternoon at Stoke City for the last game of the season. Stoke were celebrating promotion; we were on the brink of being relegated to League One for the first and only time in our history. I was as nervous then as I was on a Friday night as a player. Again, Holloway got it all wrong. He set us up defensively in the first half to contain Stoke, waiting to find out the scores from elsewhere. That was a big mistake. We stepped it up afterwards but left it too late. Relegation rivals Southampton were winning and even a draw wasn't going to be enough to save us. We bombarded Stoke during the final stages, hitting the bar and going close on several occasions only to fall short at the end. The 0-0 draw meant we were down to the third flight of English football. I was asked to do the after match phone-in but was so upset I couldn't speak. Honestly. I left the ground with my mates and went home scarcely believing things could get this bad.

As with a lot of footballers, I'd always enjoyed my golf and wasn't a bad player - at my best I was a 12 handicapper - until my fading eyesight started to take its toll – at least, that's my excuse. I'd already played a lot of golf in Spain where the sport had a thriving celebrity circuit. This was what I thought I wanted to do for a living. Truth was, of course, I hadn't made enough effort to prepare myself for life after football. Was I going to be a manager or a coach? Both appealed to me, yet apart from unsuccessfully applying for the City job and flirting with management in Non League football, I never really did the groundwork. Yes, I knew the end of my career was close. But I was in denial until the final whistle – and well beyond. I didn't get round to doing my coaching badges and I never really put myself out there as a potential manager. At the time I was best known in football at the end of a very successful, high profile career, I was in no place mentally to take the actions I needed. That proved a very costly mistake.

One of my football contacts, big Larry Lloyd, my first manager at Wigan Athletic, did me a real favour. He was working for a company selling properties out there and found a great deal for us on a spacious two-bedroom apartment, with a garden for my two Labradors and huge terrace, in Cabopino. I put all my remaining money into buying it, along with £30,000 of my mother's cash. It was a fantastic property and initially I enjoyed life there. But the fact we were unable to get an occupational licence eventually tripped me up. I was advised that it wasn't a problem and went ahead anyway. It was typical me to take chances and not go into the legal details. In the long term, this meant I couldn't sell the property. Builders promised they would get the licence to me after a few months but never did.

The truth was that Michelle was in a much better position to make the most of the move than I was. She was a very talented beauty therapist who had worked on Caribbean cruise ships and beauty was very big out there in Spain. I managed to set her up with a product called Elemis, which was quite a coup. Normally you have to be quite high up in the business to be able to get a franchise but we pulled it off after I put down a $12,000 investment bond. As I knew the owner, I managed to get Michelle a top job at the El Oceano Hotel, a high class venue. With her specialist products and the quality of the clients there, she was regularly getting 600 or 700 Euros daily in tips alone. It was not unusual for her to bring home 1,800 Euros for a day's work.

You might think that was a great way of life – and it was. Problem was I wasn't doing very well myself and it was creating a vacuum. I loved driving up and down the coast and much of Spain itself. But deep down I wasn't happy. I had been interested in golf all my life and knew people in Spain, so thought I could make a go of it. I was backed by businessman Lance Tomlyn, who chipped in £5,000 to get me a website and generally enabled me to get up and running. But I wasn't prepared to invest any more money as I was already worried about where I was heading financially. Also, I met a guy from Leicester who sold golfing holidays and worked a few days for him without being paid to learn the trade. But the doors I needed to open remained closed. There were so many companies doing golfing holidays, it was very, very difficult for a beginner like me to compete.

I was left with nothing to do other than clean the house, walk the dogs and socialise with friends and it began to get to me. I started to get depressed because I had no real purpose. It wasn't as if I was 70 years old and winding down – I still had plenty of life left in me and wanted to do something interesting with it. In addition, I was drinking every night which was the culture over there and there were plenty of friends to socialise with. Often friends came over from Leicester for holidays and I found myself out at night with them living the high life I could no longer afford. My personal hole was deepening daily even though I wasn't totally aware of it.

Marbella was a place I knew and liked very much from family holidays and thought I could make a new start there. But, as many have found out, it's one thing going to a place for short breaks, it's far different actually living there. Marbella may have had its good side but I also found it had its fair share of social problems and crooks. Cabopino itself was a great place to be in summer, but a ghost town in winter when reality started to kicked in. I began to feel very lonely after always having people around me whilst I was in football.

I came quite close to killing myself in Spain in very bizarre circumstances. It was whilst we were waiting for our house to be built and were staying at a timeshare apartment in Cabopino. One morning the front door was jammed as I was trying to get out to walk the dogs. I climbed over the outside wall and Michelle passed the dogs over to me so I could get them out. It was when I tried to get back into the house that I got into problems. Passing the dogs one by one over the wall to Michelle, the plastic chair I was standing on gave way and I skewered my stomach on the railings. I was holding myself up by my arms on the wall, knowing I was in trouble. I was very slowly slipping down, with the railing going deeper into my stomach, before I somehow summoned up the energy to spring upwards and off the railing and onto the floor into the street. I was reeling with pain and clearly in shock. I very nearly collapsed on the road, but managed to stagger on until I saw a taxi driver. He saw me and tried to wave me away, probably thinking I was going to be sick in his car. But I forced him to take me to hospital with Michelle also getting into the vehicle.

When I got there, the medics rushed out to me. They pushed Michelle away wrongly thinking she had shot me until I told them exactly what had happened. They were clearly very concerned and immediately got me ready for the operating theatre. But, fortunately for me, it was nothing like as bad as either they or I suspected. The railing had gone up rather than deeper inside my stomach and, apart from a few stitches, tidying me up and allowing the shock to subside, I was ok. I was in hospital for just a day and went home a very relieved man.

Whilst in Spain, I missed football and my former lifestyle. As a professional player, everything was provided on a plate for me. I didn't have to worry about anything from dental or doctor's appointments to hotel accommodation. Although I wasn't the best paid player in the Premier League, there weren't any money worries. The main thing I missed, though, was the banter with the lads. Watching English football on TV didn't nearly fill the gap.

I started coming home to Leicester in search of work. BMI Baby airlines row one seat A became almost as regular a slot for me as my special place on the City team coach. I still wasn't welcome at Leicester City so that wasn't an option. I was commuting every month from Spain to get work. I'd stay with David Voss, who did his best to give me a place of refuge whilst I was getting myself back on my feet. It wasn't his fault but he was winding down after a successful career in business and living a party lifestyle which only made my problems worse. It wasn't hard to see where this was all heading.

In all honesty, Michelle and I never stood a chance. I may have thought I was getting away from my problems when the truth was they were just beginning to catch up with me. My departure from Leicester, driving ban, divorce and financial worries started to hit home. One major crisis can be enough to send you off the rails, but I'd had several in a short space of time and didn't have the resources to cope any more. I was in no state to talk honestly about what was going on and instead alcohol started to get a stronger grip on me. I began to think about all the money I'd allowed to slip through my fingers and the mess I'd made of things. The eventual split ended with a massive argument which we both must regret now. Michelle, to her credit, could see it wasn't working and stayed on in the house for a short while. But, even with this, I managed to get things wrong. Without the required licence to put the property up for sale, I upped and left. It has always been a habit of mine to walk away and not face the music. I was worried I may have owed money but, equally, the opposite may well have been the case. To be honest, I still daren't ring up the bank to find out the truth – after all, it was valued at 480,000 Euros, which included my life savings, when I left. I have driven past the property since and it was boarded up. It's just one more stray piece in my jigsaw.

Returning to England in 2006 I literally had to pick my life back up from scratch. I had no property, car, cash and no life partner to share my ups and downs with. After a few more false turnings business-wise, I then had a great stroke of good fortune that has helped me turn my life around. There was something almost spooky about my first meeting with Sira, my future wife, the following year. I was in a bar in Leicester talking with a male friend when she walked in. My friend was very taken with her too. After trying to pull her with a few glasses of LPR (Laurent Perrier Rose) pink champagne (Walshy's favourite), he asked for her phone number but I was captivated. You can laugh at me, if you like, but I felt an instant connection with her as soon as she walked through the door and I'm not just talking about her physical beauty. I just felt there was chemistry between us and wanted to know more. By the end of our chat, even my friend agreed because he gave Sira's number to me!

At the time I was going out with a hairdresser called Debbie, whom David Voss had introduced me to, but, yet again, things weren't right. It ended up as a very volatile relationship with many ups and downs. Nevertheless it took a while for that fling to end in tears. In the meantime, I had what I thought was a great idea for one of my first dates with Sira. My great snooker pal Willie Thorne was doing Strictly Come Dancing and invited me down to London for the live Saturday night show. I could bring a friend and this gave me the perfect chance to phone Sira and try to impress her. Happily, she agreed and the plan was for us to pick up Willie's wife and bring her to the show.

To my surprise, when I got to his house, there were loads of media outside and Jill was in an emotional state. She had been warned there was a story appearing about Willie in the News of the World next day and was unhappy to say the least. She was reasonably ok on the way down and when the show first started, but her anger resurfaced when Willie took to the stage for his live performance. Let's just say, it was a good job the cameras didn't pan round for her reaction. As for Willie, I've never seen the great man so nervous! Next day, a mischievous article appeared about the circumstances in which the couple first got together. I couldn't believe it as it was very old news and not as bad as Jill had been expecting.

Willie wasn't the only one in trouble however. During the warm up to the show, comedian Patrick Monaghan decided to drag me onto the stage along with a 10-year-old child to do a break dance. I had a silver suit on and he called me the guy from Brokeback Mountain to make me even more embarrassed in front of my new girlfriend. Also, during the show, the cameras showed me on the front row sat next to my glamorous female companion. This came as a total shock to Debbie, who was innocently watching the TV at home having no idea I was there. When I got home, there was no point lying because I already knew where this was leading. It took a while to sort everything out, particularly as my son Nicholas was also living with us, but my heart was already set on Sira.

I can't pretend that everything slotted into place immediately and I'm so thankful to Sira that she was so patient with me and took me on, despite the baggage I was carrying. Understandably, she didn't know the deep rooted problems in my life and the dramas that inevitably came with them. My transformation came bit by bit, but it happened. I believe it's made me a better person today.

Sira is 32 years old – 17 years my junior - and now my wife and soul mate. She was born in Leicester and worked for a number of years for British Gas before taking voluntary redundancy this year because of changes to her role. She is now training to be a beautician. Some people will look at us and scoff at the age difference but we both know better. Our relationship has blossomed through all the ups and downs – largely caused by my problems.

Although I found out Sira knew a lot more about football and Leicester City than I first imagined, my lifestyle during the early stages of our courtship did shock her. My problems were too deep rooted for me to get a grip on immediately. I'd been drinking heavily for years, both during my playing days and afterwards, and there were times when I let her down pretty badly. I went off on benders and some days I could hardly get out of bed. It also took me a fair while to really open up about the full extent of my financial and personal problems and how badly my confidence had been dented. I doubted my own ability to change and get out of my rut and told Sira several times she could do a lot better. But she held on to the Walshy she believed was there somewhere below the surface and I'm unbelievably grateful for her determination today.

We were married on June 7th 2009 at Sutton Elms Church in Broughton Astley. To make the occasion even more special, I was delighted to have Bruce Nadin, the former Leicester City chaplain, taking the service. Now living in South Africa, Bruce is a great guy who does a lot of charitable work over there. It was also great to have the company and emotional support of my own dear parents and my beloved sister, who have all taken Sira to their hearts after feeling the impact of my divorce. Our family is actually quite small having seen tragedy and sadness touch our lives and that was one day when we could all celebrate. Uncle Stan's son Roy passed away suddenly in Holland in 1999 walking to a youth football match at the age of just 50. The shock was so great Auntie Marie died herself very soon afterwards. This had a tragic effect on Uncle Stan who told my parents he didn't want to live. Then Stan, who had never touched alcohol before, started drinking heavily and one night fell and banged his head against the bath and my Dad found him dead on the floor. So he got his tragic wish. All three deaths occurred within three months. I only wish they could have been there on my big day to see me so happy and the rest of the family united.

Ours was a simple wedding in a little church followed by a reception at Chris Tandy's Poachers Bistro at Thurlaston. For fine wine and food, it was always going to take a lot of beating. I've known Chris for a number of years – I call him number 22 because that was the address of the Bistro and he refers to me as number five for obvious reasons. He did a great job looking after me. I met him when he owned Henrys, a 12-seater restaurant down a little alleyway in Market Bosworth. I loved it.

The changes in my life since have been a lot to do with Sira's values; her principles and family ways have made me more aware of the need to look after my children. It's Sira's nature I connect with more than anything. With the possible exception of Michelle, who met me again at the wrong time in my life, I have never really loved someone before. The honest truth is that, until it happens, you don't really know it exists. You presume that what you have felt before was as close as it gets to the real thing but when love happens everything changes. To put it into a nutshell, love is a feeling that I would do anything for Sira. That's the way it should be. I've become much more diplomatic and able to let things go. We hardly argue at all, maybe a sign of my greater maturity. Looking back, I'm pretty sure this relationship was what I was searching for all my life whilst getting myself into all sorts of scrapes and problems.

I admit I have neglected my three children in the past and that was partly because my selfish football career came first above my kids and wife – above everything really. Now I realise that should not have been the case. In my defence, I have never turned my children away from living with me and I gave them my last pennies at a time when I was getting more and more in the financial shit. I was so fortunate Mum stood by me and gave everything she could to help me and my kids get through very difficult days. I also thank Muzzy, whom I regard as my best friend in Leicester as well as a business colleague, for his positive influence on me. He also has strong family principles and has nudged me in the right direction.

In recent years I've set out to get to know my children all over again. That's a journey that will continue for the rest of my life but I'm definitely getting there. Sons Nick and Matt both went through bad patches – but I like to think that I've helped to get them qualifications and jobs. Both are doing much better today.

Nick is aged 26 and works as a salesman for Mark's Electrical, owned by Mark Smithson, a friend of mine and a big City fan. Nick has great ability as a footballer and is a versatile player; if he had my heart and desire, he'd not be far away. Matt, 23, is almost as injury prone as I am. He has suffered some terrible injuries through sport. He left school when he was 14 when Debbie took the family to France after the break up. That was a big mistake and did nothing for his educational needs. Yet he has always been the 'lucky' one. Anything he tackles tends to turn to gold. He now works with Dave Creighton, one of the top builders in Loughborough, where he has been doing his apprenticeship and is coming on very well. He thinks he is going to be a footballer; I think he was even better at rugby. He is a fearless midfielder; infact he is fearless at everything. He certainly scares Sira and me with some of his activities. I'm equally proud of both my sons and even try to get them involved in Legends football games – recently they both scored in a 6-3 win over Forest. Get in!

Olivia, aged 21, was perhaps more convinced in the early days after the split that I was the bad guy. Now things are much better between us. It really was an awful fight for possessions and was very hurtful for me having put money into a house and not getting anything out of it and it can't have been easy for Olivia to see the truth. Academically, Olivia is the brightest of the children. She is a great girl who has worked for Melton Borough Council and is now at Kettleby Lakes, a popular holiday destination. She is quite high up and has done good work there. She is also into horses big time. We are now consciously trying to see each other more to make up for lost time. My plan over the next 15 years is to get a lot closer to all of my children.

But that's not all. For, although I didn't expect to have children with Sira, young Zaki bounced into the world about three years ago, born on July 4th 2011. This, too, came with trauma attached as Sira suffered greatly during the birth, losing a lot of blood and giving the doctors and me a big fright. Zaki Steven Walsh however is a delight. After all, I've been through – and the many, many mistakes – I feel I've been given one last and fantastic opportunity to get my family life right. Physically it has taken Sira a long time to fully recover from what happened and, to a certain extent, she is still doing so now. But, seeing Zaki in a Leicester City shirt with a number five on his back, makes me feel the future must be great for the Walsh's – all of us!

Chapter Ten

Captain's Log at 50

"

This is a battle every bit as difficult as
the physical ones I fought on a football pitch

"

WAL, as I call him, was the last of an era in so many ways. In my days, when there were no rules, we came up against a Wal or Matt Elliott every week. Everyone needed to have defenders who'd dish it out. As my friend 'Chopper' Harris told me, it would be play one, miss three (through suspension) if players like him were playing now - and it'd be the same with Wal. On the pitch, he believed in an eye for an eye and a tooth for a tooth. I'd see him run 20 or 30 yards, totally losing his position, to tell a striker exactly what he thought. Poor bloke, I knew what was coming next!

He was also the last of the 'old school' who played football and lived life. When there was no midweek match, he'd be one of seven or eight lads out on a Thursday having a 'bonding session' – we used to call it a damned good night out!

I had many a session with Wal whilst he was on the treatment table (of course) at Belvoir Drive trying to guide him to pre-plan for when he finished. I told him it's surprising how quickly it comes to an end and he needed to have something in place. He didn't listen and the truth is a very small percentage of players do plan ahead (some, of course, don't need to now because they're set up for life).

I enjoy regularly doing Q and As with Wal. We get on very well as people and always have a good laugh. He is a genuinely top bloke.

ALAN BIRCHENALL MBE, fellow Leicester City legend and Club Ambassador

I'M LUCKY enough to be still instantly recognised by Leicester City fans – and it's great. I only have to walk down the street and someone, whether I know them or not, will come up to me and share a memory from my past, either on or off the field. But, although they see the same Walshy, albeit older, broader and greyer, I know that inside I'm not the same person at all. Never will be.

I'm happier now than I've been for years but the mental scars are just as permanent as physical ones. I've been to rock bottom which I believe started with the way Tater Peeler treated me and my exit from Leicester City. From being a superman figure, Captain Fantastic, who almost thought he was invincible on a football pitch, I've woken up with no idea where to turn next. I've been torn apart through off-field problems I couldn't solve through the physical skills and bravery I had back in my day. I've felt useless, without any purpose, and wondered whether life was worth living. Yes, I can understand why some people end up taking their own lives. Instead I made a decision to fight – and I'm still fighting.

I knew life's answers were never going to be as simple as scoring another goal or winning a football match. I had to dig deeper into a mind that no longer sees things as black and white and show a different kind of strength. I'm not asking you to applaud me or give me sympathy. After all, I've got unbelievable memories to last a lifetime and I've been responsible for almost all the problems I've gone through in the last few years. I'm just telling you as it is.

Don't believe what you see. People may still look at me and think I'm physically fit for my age but have no idea of my pain. It's the same with the psychological side. I'm strong willed enough to appear confident but not in the way I was as a footballer.

Even though I have written about it as honestly as I possibly can here, the truth is you will never really get near to knowing what I went through for Leicester City over the years or how my playing days affect the way I live today. But those unfortunate enough to live with constant pain will come closer than most. Put it this way: my body gives me daily reminders of matches I shouldn't have played.

To start with, I need a new right knee; when I do something energetic, I get a pain that is almost like a knife cutting straight through it. I can no longer kneel down or squat because of all the surgery and was diagnosed with arthritis four years ago. Nigel Pearson, who knows all about it from personal experience, has recommended I have a knee replacement but I'm currently waiting as long as I can because the new joint only has a limited life span. Also, to be quite honest, I just don't fancy yet another op.

Doing something as simple and everyday as cleaning my teeth and getting downstairs is a big chore due to my dodgy knee and crushed discs in my back from the jumping and landing impact of heading a football which also causes me severe neck pain. The back pain also make it hard for me to sit still for more than a few minutes. Imagine the agony I'm in on long journeys such as flights.

That's just for starters really. There's my right hand thumb joint that dislocates frequently as a result of that injury against Palace and numerous battle scars that I can trace back to individual incidents on the pitch.

I wonder, too, about the effects of the Voltarol tablets I took orally during my last six or seven years in the game. It is an anti-inflammatory drug, which acts as a very effective short term painkiller but can't have a good long term effect on my system. Mind you, after speaking to Johnno, perhaps I'm going soft as rugby players used to take Voltarol tablets up the 'arris'.

The pain I suffer today doesn't make me bitter, but wiser. Although I don't regret the many, many times I ignored what my body was telling me and went out onto the field of battle, I'd advise today's players to listen to medical advice they are given and look after themselves. Looking back and knowing what I know now, I would never play now if I wasn't fit.

I've discovered it's impossible to fully replace the buzz you get from playing football. Those lucky enough to be managers will say being on the touchline every Saturday comes close, but only close. It's the same for me now as a fan. The best way I can explain it is a chat I had with lead singer Tom Meighan of the well known Kasabian rock band from Leicester. After one concert at De Montfort Hall, we spoke about what it feels like for him to go out in front of thousands of people and thrash out that first rock song and how similar that is to what I experienced as a player. It's an incredible adrenalin rush that makes the hairs rise up on the back of your neck. I can only describe the high as being like an innocent drug. The more you go through it, the more you want it – and the more you are bound to miss it when it's no longer possible. It wasn't just the obvious highlights like being captain of a winning team at Wembley, playing in Europe or beating top sides in the Premier League. I'm not necessarily thinking of those two goals against Derby County either. For me, getting a late winning goal against Southend United at Roots Hall and running into a crowd of Foxes fans treating the weekend like a holiday and scoring a last gasp equaliser against Arsenal in a League Cup tie at Filbert Street were just as much part of the passion of being a Leicester City player.

Well, where do I start? He is blue number five, turned number nine, Wembley winner, Derby crusher, warrior of the team; there will never ever be another Steve Walsh, I love him.

He's here, he's there, he's every fucking where - and he still is.
TOM MEIGHAN, lead singer Kasabian

If I was asked to choose my all time Leicester City team, I'd pick 11 Steve Walsh's. Put the cheque in the post!

SERGIO, from Kasabian

But what I'd really like to bring to everyone's attention is the reality of depression and anxiety, conditions that go together. Perhaps the most striking example happened four years ago when I was at home with Sira. I've had many occasions when my heart was racing but this was the worst of the lot. I was in such distress that my wife called for an ambulance. For a few minutes I honestly thought I was having a heart attack and about to die. Then I remember thinking to myself: 'Walshy, you've got to calm down and pull yourself together'. When the paramedics arrived on the scene, I was resting and feeling a little better. What I experienced was not a heart attack but a panic attack, an extremely frightening experience I don't ever want to go through again.

I was on antidepressants for six months about two years ago. But citalopram, a commonly prescribed drug for depression and anxiety, didn't work for me. It probably didn't help that I was still drinking. You think having alcohol will distract you from your problems but when you wake up next day you find you're actually feeling worse, not better. At one point I was in a very lethargic state in which I was happy enough to sleep rather than face everyday life.

Eventually I went to see a counsellor in Nottingham to talk about my problems. I came to the conclusion I needed to sort my own life out rather than leave it to someone else or medication. In my view, depression existed inside my own head and no tablet nor professional person could solve it for me.

This, I believe, is a battle every bit as difficult as the physical ones I fought on a football pitch. It's easier to appreciate recovering from a broken leg when you can see physical improvement; not so easy to recognise the mental fight that goes on inside a mind. But that doesn't make it any less real. Depression is something I'll probably have to deal with for years, or even for the rest of my life. I naturally get tense and anxious when things are going wrong and that gets me down. Depression among current and former sportsmen and women is a subject that has been brought more to public attention in recent years and that is a positive thing.

There's no point beating about the bush – my current involvement in football, particularly with my good friend and former City colleague Muzzy Izzet, is great, but in some ways I still feel a failure. Not everyone would agree I'm management material, but I know I could have done it. I honestly believe I have the football knowledge to have made it as either a manager or a coach and nobody is ever going to doubt my enthusiasm and passion. It all goes back, I suppose, to when I applied for the City job with Tony Cottee. Yes, there were good reasons why we didn't get the post after Martin O'Neill left – not least the fact that neither of us had any managerial experience nor the coaching badges. But ask me the question whether we could have held that dressing room together and taken Leicester City forward and the answer is 'yes'. A lot of the X-Factor that makes a good manager comes from the relationship with the players. We hear all the time about managers losing the dressing room and players not performing for a particular boss – and it's true. That extra mile between drawing and winning a match often comes down to the bond between the manager and players crossing the white line. We were more than happy to put bodies, souls, everything on the line for Martin O'Neill. He moulded us together as one and made us stronger than the individual abilities of all of us combined.

The mistake I made, is one I now tell young people over and over again to avoid – I didn't react in the right way. I honestly believe I've wasted a lot of the last 10 years, particularly when I went to Spain. I should have gone back to grass roots and started at the bottom like Martin did. Instead I failed to do the two things to bridge the gap between having the enthusiasm to do the job – and actually doing it. I didn't get myself qualified with my coaching badges and I didn't put myself in the shop window. Instead I had a short time working with my mate Gary Mills at Tamworth and jacked it in when the Grantham farce returned to bite me. So I buggered off to Spain and let precious years slip by when I was still very well known in the game.

Should I get a chance to put that lost opportunity right, I'd surprise a few people. I may have been a firebrand on the pitch, remembered as much for my sendings off as my football by some folk, but that wouldn't be the way I'd manage. I've learned enough from the FA courses I have attended in recent years to know jumping up and down on the touchline contesting every decision and handing out regular bollockings isn't the way forward. I'd take a leaf out of the book of current City manager Nigel Pearson. Everyone knows he's a passionate man – a hard tackling defender in his day and quite capable of dishing it out as a manager. But he has learned a different way of handling the pressure and Leicester City benefited from that during our fantastic title winning season. I would have loved to have played under him, that's for certain. That comment is not made out of sentiment but having watched the way his teams play the game, his relationship with the players and backroom staff is second to none. Nigel is a top, top man in my view and has to be one of the best managers in the history of the club.

Firstly, he took the 'bad times' towards the end of the 2012/13 season when we slipped from leading the Championship to just squeezing into the play offs on the final day at Forest in his stride. Publicly, at least, he never lost his resolve or confidence in the players and, crucially, the Foxes board never lost their belief in him. Whilst countless other clubs have chopped and changed their manager several times in recent seasons, City stuck with a good man and he and his squad took the lessons from the heartbreak of a traumatic play off semi final defeat at Watford and turned it to our advantage. There were raised eyebrows last season when Nigel was seen watching the team from the stand rather than patrolling the touchline, but he knew what he was doing. From there, he actually has a far better view, in certain ways, of what is going on than on the touchline and can spot the two or three things he can then pass onto the players at half time.

We've learned a huge amount through sports science in recent years, not least the psychological side of the game. Eating, drinking and socialising to excess was part and parcel of the sport in England in my day. Most of us did it and enjoyed it and still went out there and performed on a Saturday. But now we have learned more about nutrition, the way the body recovers after an intense 90 minutes and the importance of a healthy lifestyle, we know better. If I had my time again, I'd do it differently because I could never have got away with being part of the Thursday night club and tackling today's ultra fit strikers less than 48 hours later. It's the same with the mind. I took my fair share of bollockings and mostly took them on the chin. That's the way it was during my playing days. But is that the best way to motivate all footballers? From what the FA has taught me – including amazing and very eye-opening stuff on the way most of us tick – the answer is no. Instead we need to find a happy medium. There is still a place for an old fashioned telling off at the right time but good managers and coaches aren't necessarily the ones who shout the loudest but those who get their points across and taken on board by the players. That's a far different art form.

Instead of being a manager or a coach, I'm doing the next best thing working with young people – including some of the players of tomorrow – through the soccer academy I run with Muzzy. It was my good luck when I returned from Spain to sit down with Muzzy and chat about what we could do. I always thought we would make a good business partnership because we were good friends as well as team mates from our City days and have mutual respect for what we have achieved in the past and can give to other people now. Muzzy was a terrific footballer who grabbed his chance when brought to Leicester from Chelsea's reserves; he won honours with us and with his country, including coming on as a substitute in the 2002 World Cup semi final when Turkey lost 1-0 to eventual champions Brazil. Between us, we've got the football pitch covered. I was the hard tackling and heading defender who fancied himself as a striker; he was the box-to-box endless energy and skilful midfielder managers dream of having in their side. Muzzy had everything. Between us, there isn't much we haven't experienced or know about when it comes to football.

Muzzy has become a very good friend. Without doubt, he was the best Leicester City player I ever played with - Lenny, Elliott and Heskey running him a close second. Off the pitch, Muzzy has great family beliefs and values and has helped me to learn about my own domestic life. It was a real shame that Muzzy's career ended fairly early at the age of 32 through a knee injury; otherwise he could have played for another five years. He was a key part of that famous midfield of Izzet, Lennon and Savage, who was closely pushed by Garry Parker. Muzzy played alongside former Arsenal and France star Robert Pires and Robbie in a charity match hosted by One Direction star Niall Horan at the King Power Stadium on Bank Holiday Monday earlier this year and looked so good he could probably still play at the top level now but for his knee. As for me, I lasted 30 minutes also playing for TV personality Piers Morgan's side – that was more than enough for me.

We share a passion for Leicester City. Neither of us come from Leicester originally, but both regard the Foxes as our club. We live locally and are desperate to see the club do well. Therefore we set up the Steve Walsh and Muzzy Izzet Soccer Academy with the aim, not only of helping local youngsters, aged from five to 14, but producing 'Future Foxes' for Leicester City.

We have enjoyed working in many schools in and around Leicestershire and continue to do a lot of charity work in the local community. One school we have a particularly close relationship with is Castle Rock High School in Coalville, where we run a six-week rewards programme called 'Positive Choices'. We begin by introducing the youngsters to our own careers in a question and answer session and go on to host sports activities and offer nutritional advice. The programme is designed to build confidence among young people suffering from low self esteem. We end with a presentation at Leicester City Football Club including a stadium tour. We've been doing this for around four years and it has proved a huge success. It's great for both of us to see the difference we can make in the life of a young person through football.

Muzzy and I are among the regular coaches. Already our academy has yielded three or four players who have gone onto the books of Leicester City and this is something we are proud of and want to build on. We believe we are there to help recruit players to the Foxes. We have the same philosophy as Leicester City's academy to produce players comfortable on the ball and able to pass it out from the back and through the 'thirds' of the pitch. Gone are the days of hitting Row Z – which I was so good at! - it's important to get the ball down now and retain possession.

I'm very excited that the club's academy now has EPPP1 category 'A' status. It's great that the Under 21's team is winning trophies and competing with the best youngsters in the land. The biggest clubs will always cherry pick players at youth level but for us to be competing with them is a fantastic achievement. Clubs like Leicester City have simply got to produce their fair share of home grown players if we are going to thrive, particularly in an era where Financial Fair Play is set to punish those who spend money they don't earn. Only a few years ago we were losing promising youngsters to the likes of Forest and West Brom, today the boot is on the other foot. Already we've seen Liam Moore, Andy King , Conrad Logan and Jeff Schlupp make it through the ranks and into the City first team and, with the set up we have now, I confidently expect more to follow.

We've been running our own academy for more than six years and, as I'm writing, we have just begun a very exciting new project called AFDA (Advanced Football Development Academy) based at Blaby and Whetstone Boys Club with partners PTC Sports, from Sheffield. We also have a kind sponsorship relationship with Walker Bros, a branch of Samworth Brothers. We are working with 16 to 18-year-olds on a joint football and educational programme which gives them a pathway either into the professional game or employment within sport. Altogether this year we are working with 55 young people out of an incredible 300-plus applicants; 45 have been carefully selected to do BTEC Level 2 and 3 courses in sport with the remaining ten apprentices studying for their coaching badges. Some have been cast aside by professional clubs and we are there to keep their dream alive. Our ultimate goal is to unearth young talent for the professional game but the football side is balanced with academic and vocational qualifications and life skills to help them to become a success in any field. The interest has been so great that we are already in talks about opening another centre elsewhere in the county.

When I first walked into the Leicester City dressing room, there were some big characters there but Walshy was the biggest of all – he was club captain and our leader on and off the pitch. He introduced himself and told me he'd be there if I needed anything. Playing in front of him, I could see his attributes on the pitch. The relationship between central defenders and central midfielders has to be good – and it was. We had a very good spine in that side. Walshy may have lost it with opponents sometimes but he was actually very calm and respectful in the way he spoke with us and gave us advice on the field. He was almost like a father figure to us. Lenny and I were young and could get about the pitch whilst Walshy marshalled the back and swept up anything that got into our box. He was a physical player and that rubbed off on us as a team. I loved every second playing for Leicester City; we were often underdogs and up against it, but nearly always came through.

I met up again with Walshy after he came back from Spain. I was thinking about setting up a football academy and he was too. So we chatted and decided to work together. We're completely different people – Walshy is more tense and wants things done straightaway whilst I'm more laid back, but we are good for each other.

It's great to now be working with Walshy on a new challenge through our AFDA programme. Between us we have a wealth of football knowledge and want to share it. There is undiscovered talent out there and, if we can push anyone City's way in future, all the better.

On a personal side, Walshy has suffered several setbacks in his life since his playing days including divorce and bankruptcy. Even to this day, I instantly know when Walshy is down or not feeling great. I'd imagine his depression is something that will be with him a long time but the happier he is, the less that will be an issue. He has married again, has a young son and his work with the academy and elsewhere is coming together. Walshy is in a better place again now which is good to see.

We're both delighted Leicester are back in the Premier League. The team is entering the unknown – just like we did in our day – and it's going to be tough and exciting.

By MUZZY IZZET, Leicester City player 1996-2004

My love affair with Leicester City may seem strange to anyone who doesn't follow us. After all, I was brought up in Lancashire and only came to Filbert Street to further my own ambitions. But to fellow Foxes, or true supporters of any other team for that matter, it makes total sense. It's something many players will never experience and I think they're missing out. They get shipped from club to club and, although human nature means almost all of them will give 100 per cent on the field, they don't really share the passion off it.

I'm really thrilled to feel part of Leicester City all over again – and a lot of the credit needs to go to Nigel Pearson and the new owners. My involvement with the club is increasing all the time. I don't have a title but I have an ambassador-like role. My main work is in hospitality at all our home games. I host one particular room hosting more than 100 match day guests. I start a couple of hours before kick off, meeting and greeting and sharing some old time favourite banter whilst they enjoy a three-course meal. Highlights include Birch bringing in the team sheet and a visit from a City player who is not in the side that day. I watch the game with fellow Leicester legends Ali Mauchlen, Ian Marshall and Matt Elliott and then do a post-match chat discussing the game with the guests. Then it's off on the piss if we've won – or stay in, with the hump, if we haven't Some things never change!

Altogether I'm thrilled my relationship with the club has been fully restored since the new owners took over. Chief executive Susan Whelan and chairman Vichai Srivaddhanaprabha and his family have made me feel more than welcome again – and part of the City furniture. Manager Nigel Pearson has also been unbelievable with me, inviting me down to the training ground and always making a point of speaking to me.

I have been in a good position to see what the new owners have done for my football club, some of which won't be so obvious to all City fans. I honestly believe that they have achieved a lot more than helping to provide us with a winning team. The way they are building the club, they are giving us the right foundations to enjoy success for years to come. Part of this is their very enthusiastic backing for our academy and at the training ground. This summer alone they have spent a small fortune developing Belvoir Drive with replica pitches to the King Power Stadium and generally upgrading the facilities. No expense has also been spared in making sure our stadium is in tip top condition for the Premier League. I have seen with my own eyes their amazing attention to detail – everything they do speaks of perfection.

The owners have also been very supportive of the community in general, backing many charities and taking over what was previously a shambles of a Football in the Community programme now creating positive links with schools. Again, this doesn't affect how we get on next Saturday but is all about building Leicester City's fan base and our place in the community as a whole. It's also a very good sign that they are as good as their word and are here for the long haul. Altogether they have answered all the understandable questions that are always raised when foreign owners take control of an English club – I couldn't be happier with them in charge.

Walshy on the fans: "I've always felt at home with City fans because I'm one of them. They supported me fantastically on the pitch and looked after me off it whilst I was a player. Today there is nothing better than watching Leicester City away games for atmosphere. Being right among the supporters is amazing. My trips with Ross Greaves, from D and J Catering, were brilliant times. He looked after me big time with his John – we got meat and potato pies from every ground we went.

"The atmosphere at Filbert Street was unique because it was an intimate ground and we made it a very intimidating place for some of the best teams in the land, particularly during the Martin O'Neill days. The King Power is definitely one of the best of the 'new' grounds and I'd encourage our fans to raise the roof as much as possible. The atmosphere against Everton in the first game of this season was incredible. Away from home, too, Leicester City fans are as vocal as anyone. You really can be our 12th man in the Premier League."

Media-wise I'm busy. It's been a pleasure working with the Sky Sports team summarising a number of City games. This season I've just launched my new i Tunes podcast featuring interviews with Leicester City legends and other special guests.

I also enjoy question and answer nights with Gerry Taggart, Ian Marshall and Matt Elliott but, more frequently, with The Birch, Alan Birchenall. The two of us form a very good double act. We're both extrovert characters who are very popular with the fans and enjoy the banter. We bounce off each other particularly well and usually have a good crack.

It's difficult to take in that I'll be 50 years old when you are reading this. I'm sure you'll agree I've packed a lot into my years but, on the other hand, time seems to have flown by. If you think I deliberately timed my autobiography to co-incide with being 50, City being back in the Premier League and the 20th anniversary of that unforgettable Wembley day against Derby, you're probably giving me too much credit. To be honest, I couldn't have written that story if I'd tried.

I must admit it saddens me that there will probably never be another Steve Walsh or Matt Elliott at Leicester City in the future. We were, as Birchy rightly says, part of a last generation of footballers who played and socialised hard. Whereas we set out to win the physical battle with strikers, it's a far different challenge for defenders in today's game. They have to stay on their feet and avoid the sort of challenge cunning strikers so easily turn into a free kick or a penalty. Plus, of course, they need to be much more comfortable on the ball and retain possession. Ironically, the nearest to a Walshy in the game is probably our own Wes Morgan, the current Leicester City captain. There is old fashioned physicality in his game but, as our fans know, he can play a bit as well.

It's so different off the field as well. For, although today's footballers are publicised and idolised far more than in my playing days, they don't have the same connection with the fans. It's not their fault but the social culture we had at Leicester City is now a thing of the past. Most of today's players prepare for matches as elite professionals as sports science has made everyone much more aware of the need to nurture minds and bodies. Makes me smile when I think of my room mate Matt Elliott with his feet up in a hotel room smoking away the night before a game. In all, we had seven smokers in the squad that won two League Cups!

The part of football that will never change is the passion of real fans. It might seem barmy to unbelievers that we go through such an emotional rollercoaster every time our team plays – but I would never be without it, that's for sure. Watching the Foxes win a football match is still one of the most enjoyable things in my life, all the more so because of the bond I have always felt with you, the fans.

I'm really pleased to say that I'm feeling a whole lot better these days. I've emerged from the dark place in which I found myself after leaving Leicester City and now have a much clearer sense of purpose and direction once again. The excesses that caused me so many problems in the past are now under control at last. I'm a much better person with the love and support of Sira and my whole family.

But I couldn't have done it without the fantastic relationship I have with fellow Leicester City supporters. You've been there through the red cards, the injuries and Wembley heartbreaks through to scoring last minute goals, silencing The Rams, our brilliant seasons in the Premier League, winning League Cups and that amazing night in Madrid. I may have done many things I regret in my life – not all of which you'll find in these pages! - but, not for one second, do I regret the incredible journey I've shared with all of you – and continue to share today.

As I'm writing our Premier League adventure is just beginning. There was something familiar about scoring so late on against Everton on opening day and I was also a guest at Stamford Bridge where we put up such a really good performance at title favourites Chelsea. It looks as if Nigel Pearson has bought well in the summer and we can compete again in the top league.

I'm sure City fans would agree that it feels like the Martin O'Neill days all over again. Nigel has built the same close feeling within the team and we are becoming a team that even the big boys worry about once again as our performances against Arsenal and, even more spectacularly, Manchester United have shown. My final game before going into print is already being spoken of as the greatest City game ever as we came back from 3-1 down to humble United 5-3 and that's saying something after my great battles with Arsenal, Derby and Fulham to name just three.

The United triumph highlighted, for me, what Leicester City have always been about – you can knock us down as many times as you want, but we will always come back fighting.

I am proud of all our lads in a City shirt but you'll forgive me I'm sure for devoting my final word to young Liam Moore – it's great to see a young man who has come through our academy in the centre of our defence against some of the best strikers in the world. As fellow fans sing he truly is 'one of our own' and I happily admit to feeling a touch of envy that his City journey is just beginning.

You know what, if I had my life all over again, I wouldn't change a fucking thing. Except perhaps I would land that famous Walshy elbow on Tater Peeler's bugle!

Keep the faith! Up the City, we hate Forest, down with the Sheepshaggers and here's to the next 50 years (in the Premier League, of course).

Thanks Nigel and the boys for a happy ending!

Special acknowledgements, I would like to thank:

My family: Mum, Dad, Susan, Neil, Hannah and Alex for their unconditional love and supporting me through the best and worst times in my life.

My children: Nick, Matt and Olivia for letting me rebuild our relationship we should never have lost. I love you all very much.

Sira my wife for pulling me through some of the toughest years of my life and the pain she went through to give us a very special little boy Zaki.

My Kkong Events partner Shane Whitfield for helping me to make this book happen.

Muzzy Izzet for his loyal support.

John Brindley for writing this book and listening to my stories over and over again.

Good friend Kevin Bourgault for all the long hours, Spectrum Printing Services Ltd and NX Logistics Ltd for their kind distribution.

Leicester Mercury.

Neil Plumb (Plumb Images).

Adam Gillott at Three Point Design for creating some fantastic artwork.

And finally my devoted loyal LCFC fans who remained by my side all the way through this rollercoaster ride I will never forget!!